Engaging Community through Storytelling

Engaging Community through Storytelling

Library and Community Programming

SHERRY NORFOLK AND JANE STENSON,
EDITORS

Foreword by Carol Birch

LIBRARIES
UNLIMITED™

An Imprint of ABC-CLIO, LLC
Santa Barbara, California • Denver, Colorado

Library of Congress Cataloging-in-Publication Data

Names: Norfolk, Sherry, 1952- editor. | Stenson, Jane, 1941- editor.
Title: Engaging community through storytelling : library and community
   programming / Sherry Norfolk and Jane Stenson, editors ; foreword
   by Carol Birch.
Description: Santa Barbara, California : Libraries Unlimited, an imprint of
   ABC-CLIO, LLC, [2017] | Includes bibliographical references and index.
Identifiers: LCCN 2017016636 (print) | LCCN 2017025452 (ebook) | ISBN
   9781440850707 (ebook) | ISBN 9781440850691 (hardcopy : acid-free paper)
Subjects: LCSH: Libraries and community. | Storytelling. | Libraries—
   Activity programs. | Libraries—Activity programs—United States—Case studies.
Classification: LCC Z716.4 (ebook) | LCC Z716.4 .E54 2017 (print) |
   DDC 027.62/51—dc23
LC record available at https://lccn.loc.gov/2017016636

ISBN: 978–1–4408–5069–1
EISBN: 978–1–4408–5070–7

21 20 19 18 17   1 2 3 4 5

This book is also available as an eBook.

Libraries Unlimited
An Imprint of ABC-CLIO, LLC

ABC-CLIO, LLC
130 Cremona Drive, P.O. Box 1911
Santa Barbara, California 93116-1911
www.abc-clio.com

This book is printed on acid-free paper ∞

Manufactured in the United States of America

This book is dedicated to the *storytelling community*—the whole richly diverse, open-minded, generous-spirited, and creative lot of you, who understand exactly what Rudyard Kipling meant in *The Second Jungle Book* (1895) when he said, "The strength of the wolf is the pack, and the strength of the pack is the wolf."

You are our pack, and we gain strength and inspiration from you.
—Sherry Norfolk and Jane Stenson

Contents

Foreword ix
Carol Birch

Acknowledgments xiii

Introduction xv
Sherry Norfolk and Jane Stenson

1. **Voices for Intercultural Understanding** 1

Transforming Society through Youth Storytelling:
    Children at the Well 2
Paula Weiss

Social Justice Storytelling Then and Now 14
Susan O'Halloran

Multicultural Family Adventures in Reading 21
Onawumi Jean Moss

Building International Community through Storytelling............. 23
Dr. Aaron Wills and Dr. Lisa Overholser with Sherry Norfolk

All for Stories—All for Education: Creating a Place
    for Intergenerational Knowledge in the Classroom 37
Lillian Rodrigues Pang

2. **Voices of Our Elders** 49

Elders Tell 50
Lynn Rubright

The Elders Circle 54
Jim May

Weaving Community 58
Cherri Coleman

3. **Voices of Cultural Pride** 65

Storytellers as Community Cultural Ambassadors 66
Karen Abdul-Malik a.k.a. Queen Nur

Becoming Visible through Our Stories.............................. 77
Nancy Wang

Building Community through Cultural Storytelling.................. 82
Rose McGee

4. Voices of Students of All Ages 89

Creating Community through a College-Based Storytelling
Program: The Storytelling Institute at South Mountain
Community College 91
Liz Warren

Enriching Minds, Encouraging Hope and Joy: Columbus Story
Adventures—a Community-Outreach Program of the
Storytellers of Central Ohio...................................... 102
Lyn Ford

Taking the Stage: The Lone Star Student Storyteller Program 109
*Bonnie Barber, Cindy Boatfield, Lisa Bubert, Julie Chappell,
Jennifer Cummings, and Mayra Diaz*

The National Youth Storytelling Showcase......................... 123
Nannette Watts

Heritage Night: School Programming 127
Jane Stenson

5. Voices of the Disenfranchised 133

Crossroads: Stories for Reaching At-Risk Youth.................... 134
Lorna MacDonald Czarnota

The Power of Creative Story for Alzheimer's Patients and
Those with Other Special Needs 141
Pete and Joyce Vanderpool

Storytelling in the Addiction Recovery Community 147
Gene and Peggy Helmick-Richardson

Bibliography.. 155

Index... 159

About the Editors and Contributors 165

Foreword

Carol Birch

It is beyond the scope of this foreword to explore how profound loneliness and isolation splinters communities in the twenty-first century, but consider two images. Rollo May, in *The Cry for Myth*, identified a fierce independence imbedded in the myths of the New World and Wild West as American archetypal myths. The "Marlboro Man" might epitomize that *idealized independent man alone and rootless moving into vast empty spaces.* Contrast this isolated individual with the image of the storytelling circle in which those delving into *story* are implicitly and explicitly linked. The storytelling journey moves through *time, for stories are rooted in the past and grow out of culture, ethnicity, religion, history, folk wisdom, identity, information, and experience.*

In this book, you will read about people who create circles of *stories to support* their communities. You will even find model storytelling projects that are *literally creating communities through stories* both nationally and internationally. This diverse array of projects originates in libraries, community centers, schools, and churches—anywhere that people gather, and anywhere people care to connect, educate, or entertain one another. As a former librarian/storyteller, I am naturally excited about storytelling projects in public libraries. I view libraries and storytelling through prisms of possibility for community programming. *Engaging Community through Storytelling: Library and Community Programming* is an invitation to view storytelling projects through whatever prism is your own—they form a kaleidoscope of potential for growing community!

* * *

In 2000, four friends, appalled by escalating violence in their community, initiated a program where people gathered to hear stories of the "other" at a festival in Copenhagen. They named it "The Human Library." It was based on the belief violence diminishes when we have heard stories that humanize those we have hated, feared, reviled, or ostracized. Those friends in Denmark recognized what the authors of this book, its contributors, and early librarians all know: storytelling builds bridges of understanding within the human psyche and between human beings.

At the end of the nineteenth century as public libraries established rooms devoted to books published for children, legendary librarians like

Anne Carroll Moore of the New York Public Library promoted services to attract children and their families into the library. Storytelling featured prominently in programming offered right from the start. Astounded by the artistry of Marie Shedlock, an actress and storyteller from England, Ms. Moore incorporated training in storytelling during salaried hours for librarians. Just as importantly, Ms. Moore invited immigrant parents and grandparents to add their voices and tales to the array of stories for children to hear. A hundred years later with little fanfare, libraries continue to support and extend their reach to the community with storytelling programs staffed by librarians, guest storytellers within the community, and the occasional platform storytellers.*

Storytelling deepens the emotional affinity and the actual rapport among people as it encourages the development of empathy, courage, compassion, and even a sense of humor. As Newbery award-winning author Kate DiCamillo asserts, authors "have been given *the sacred task of making hearts large through story*." Librarians/storytellers offer programs to connect children to those heart-expanding stories. Yes, the stories may be housed in books, in the people of a community, in a special guest; they might be read or told *out loud* one-on-one or in programs by a storytelling librarian.

Like many librarians, before earning a graduate degree in library *service* (not library *science*), I worked at the circulation desk of a library. My job was to track down overdue books. My experience of libraries focused exclusively on library-as-store-house-of-books with the laughable goal of securing every book to a shelf, of course, in the correct place! Graduate school exploded such a narrow definition of library service into something closer to Caitlin Moran's exuberant view:

> *A library in the middle of a community is a cross between an emergency exit, a life raft and a festival. They are cathedrals of the mind; hospitals of the soul; theme parks of the imagination. On a cold, rainy island, they are the only sheltered public spaces where you are not a consumer, but a citizen, instead.*

A citizen of the world, I would add! No ID card is required to enter a public library and access its vast array of resources. In the words of Neil Gaiman: "Libraries are not child-care facilities, but sometimes *feral children raise themselves* among the stacks."

Intellectual freedom is a fundamental aspect of democracy; it is also assiduously promoted in graduate programs in library education. Historically the American Library Association opposed the PATRIOT Act's intrusive requirement that librarians keep records of their patrons. Library education is inclusive, promoting the principles of unity in diversity. Storyteller, school librarian, and recipient of the National Storytelling Network's Story Bridge Award for her work in Namibia among the Ju/'hoansi, Melissa Heckler envisions libraries as arks carrying the hopes of democracy. She says, "When things go crazy, libraries hold fast to the dream! Libraries are literally safe havens getting us through the stormy seas of today."

Stories blossom in relationships; relationships blossom in stories. A children's librarian/storyteller enjoys satisfactions that grow out of and reinforce relationship, continuity, and community. Over the years, a unique and personal relationship develops between librarians and patrons; it grows with every formal and informal story shared. The local librarian/storyteller becomes one of the "benign adults," so valuable in a child's development. Studies demonstrate that the presence of "non-parental adult role models is significant for youth in discovering leadership. Non-parental adult role models extend opportunities and provide support and encouragement." Librarians/storytellers enjoy the unequaled pleasure of watching a child grow from a "sack-of-potato-infant" to a toddler who masters the skills of clapping and singing to elementary-age children involved in active listening. To witness this miraculous transformation gets many a librarian/storyteller up in the morning with a smile.

Wearing the story-hat releases librarians and youth from boundaries imposed by the demands of formal instruction and discipline. The bond between them grows as shared reference points deepen—almost—into a sense of shared ancestry. This continuity is invaluable, for it invites a spontaneity and playfulness that can only flourish among those with prior shared experiences. Libraries—with their extraordinary staffs, physical space, commitment to intellectual freedom, and free access to information in extensive print and nonprint resources—can bring people together to enhance both community life and the lives of individuals within that community. As Catherynne M. Valente says:

> *A Library...should positively vibrate with laughing at comedies and sobbing at tragedies, it should echo with gasps as decent ladies glimpse indecent things and indecent ladies stumble upon secret and scandalous decencies! A Library should not shush; it should roar!*

While mass media continue to portray librarians in distinctly unattractive ways, authors often describe librarians as a positive force within their communities and in their lives. Marilyn Johnson praises them as "information professionals, teachers, police, community organizers, computer technicians, historians, confidantes, clerks, social workers, storytellers, or...guardians of [her] peace."

Just as I once thought of a library as a storehouse for books and grew to understand its wider role as an information and community service organization, so too I came to understand the vitality of storytelling in the library extends far beyond of its formal programs. People enter libraries to better prepare for joyful occasions or frightening challenges they, or loved ones, face. And they talk—libraries resound with informal story swaps in hushed tones or exuberant ones. Patrons tell their stories to one another and to the library staff. The importance of actual library buildings cannot be overstated. Libraries provide places to congregate. During 9/11 or when emergencies strike local communities, libraries often remain open so people can gather to find comfort in community.

Let us hear it for library storytelling circles weaving together a community among disparate patrons by some alchemical process of mixing the personal with the ancient. Preschool-age children through young adults might share a breathless silence or raucous laughter over human foibles and triumphs found in stories. Hopefully, one and all most often depart the library feeling less isolated or lonely, refreshed by a shared experience that has reinforced their sense of community. Stories paradoxically enlarge a sense of possibility even as they lead us home.

***Note:** I prefer "platform" to "professional" storyteller. Professional is often equated with the financial independence of freelance artists; there is nothing unprofessional about librarians and others whose salaried work includes storytelling.

Bibliography

DiCamillo, Kate. Newbery acceptance speech on June 29, 2014, at the American Library Association Annual Conference.

Gaiman, Neil. Excerpt from Gaiman's 2009 Newbery Medal acceptance speech, http://www.goodreads.com/quotes/617290-reading-is-important-books-are-important-librarians-are-important-also.

Human Library. http://humanlibrary.org/about-the-human-library/#S06zzs65uRSYxDHA.99.

Johnson, Marilyn. *This Book Is Overdue!* New York: Harper Perennial, 2011, 252.

Moran, Caitlyn. *Moranthology*. New York: Harper Perennial, 2012, 160.

Rishel, C., S. Esther, and G. F. Koeske. "Relationships with Non-Parental Adults and Child Behavior." *Child and Adolescent Social Work Journal* 22, no. 1 (February 2005).

Rollo May. *The Cry for Myth*. New York: W.W. Norton, 1991, 93–100.

Valente, Catherynne M. *The Girl Who Soared over Fairyland and Cut the Moon in Two*. New York: Feiwel & Friends, 2013, 10.

Acknowledgments

We wish to thank the following:

- The National Storytelling Network for its support of applied storytelling with the Brimstone Award, which has provided funding for community-building storytelling projects worldwide.
- The countless people who said, "you should talk to..." and "have you heard about..." and "surely you know about..." You expanded our horizons, informed our thinking, and enriched this book.
- The community venues—libraries, community centers, churches, and synagogues who open your doors and hearts to storytelling.
- Bobby, for his patience in allowing me to process this book—endlessly!—out loud. Thank you for always listening!
- Andrew and Lily—you represent the youth of the world who, through their participation, reap the benefits of community storytelling.

Introduction

Sherry Norfolk and Jane Stenson

No matter what people tell you, words and ideas can change the world.
   —Robin Williams in *Dead Poets Society* (1989)

Changing the world—one person, one story, one community at a time: that is what this book is about. It is about exploring ways to bring people together by listening to each other's stories. It is about maximizing our humanity.

Why stories and storytelling? Because "we are social animals and storytelling is the empathetic tie that binds us to one another with bands of steel" (Deedy 2014). Stories are an essential part of our humanity—they identify and connect us with our human family.

Barbara Ganley, founder and director of Community Expressions LLC, writes that "story is what distinguishes humans from all of our mammalian relatives, distant and close. It is the glue that binds hearts, souls and minds, and it is the force that can heal wounds between and among individuals and communities. It is the light that sparks mutual understanding and respect, which in turn fuel positive, collective action" (Ganley 2010).

In this book, we have the opportunity to see the inner workings of a wide variety of model storytelling projects from across the country, each providing a fascinating glimpse into how storytelling is being used in community work in libraries, community centers, schools, homeless shelters, synagogues, and churches to encourage community attachment, identity, and expression.

Choose your corner, pick away at it carefully, intensely and to the best of your ability and that way you might change the world.
   —Charles Eames

Each of these projects has been carefully designed to meet the specific needs of a particular purpose—its "corner"—and employs storytelling as the ultimate tool to change hearts and lives: to change the world. Simply recognizing the number and scope of the community-building storytelling projects in this country is astonishing; the depth and breadth of the work is humbling and inspiring.

And here is what else is astonishing: in the spirit of community, the remarkable people who designed and implemented these stunning projects are willing and eager to share the nuts and bolts of their creative visions with you! In these articles, they explain where they got the ideas, the support, the funding, and the stamina to persevere—sometimes against rather daunting odds. In addition, they provide insights into how to avoid the pitfalls and what to do when (inevitably) a pitfall is unavoidable.

In other words, they each provide a how-to-do-it guide to encourage and enable your replication of their hard work!

We are extremely grateful to them for their generosity, and we are optimistic that you will be inspired to develop your own community-building storytelling project ASAP!

Organization of This Book

We have organized our chapters by target audience. Why? Because each of the programs described in this book is defined by its laser focus on meeting the specific needs of a specific group of people. Venues are changeable: the location in which a particular project has been conducted is not the *only* place in which that sort of work can be done. A program sponsored by a church can be offered in a library or school with only a few modifications and a little imagination—but a project that targets runaway teens is not likely to succeed with elders, or vice versa.

Who do you want to reach? What corner will you choose?

Chapter 1: Voices for Intercultural Understanding

Paula Weiss writes about the **Children at the Well**, a storytelling program that helps young people tap into the richness of stories from their traditions to increase their understanding of and appreciation for diversity, to increase their empathy for others, and to enhance their own self-discovery and development of voice.

Susan O'Halloran writes about **Social Justice Storytelling Then and Now**, examining her collaboration with Father Derek Simons and the Society of the Divine Word that has produced 20 years of community-based live, online, and media-driven storytelling projects.

In **Multicultural Family Adventures in Reading**, Onawumi Jean Moss describes a vibrant community library program.

Building International Community through Storytelling, by Dr. Aaron Wills and Dr. Lisa Overholser with Sherry Norfolk, describes the Starlight Goodwill Ambassador Educational and Cultural Program, through which a team of Taiwanese youth tellers participate in an American storytelling festival, attend an American school for several days, and homestay with American families. The American and Taiwanese students share insights about each other's cultures—and make lasting friendships!

In **All for Stories—All for Education: Creating a Place for Intergenerational Knowledge in the Classroom**, Lillian Rodrigues Pang details a rich interweaving of generations and cultures through storytelling.

Chapter 2: Voices of Our Elders

Lynn Rubright recounts a rich array of experiences and settings in her article, **Elders Tell**, as elders tell their stories (at churches, schools, libraries, and community and cultural centers).

Jim May describes developing and nurturing **The Elders Circle**, which encourages elders to share their life experience stories on a regular basis throughout the year, with the goal of helping these elders develop improved communication and socialization skills and self-esteem.

In her article, **Weaving Community**, Cherri Coleman vividly describes her experiences at Historic Rock Castle in Hendersonville, Tennessee, where storytelling and basket weaving created a sense of community between three generations.

Chapter 3: Voices of Cultural Pride

"Storytelling is the heart of cultural sustainability…stories project images of collective experiences, and contain the quintessence of creation-…the rhythm of life," says Queen Nur in her article, **Storytellers as Community Cultural Ambassadors**.

In **Becoming Visible through Our Stories**, Nancy Wang explores ways in which Eth-Noh-Tec is positively impacting the visibility and pride of the Asian American community while developing cross-cultural connections.

Building Community through Cultural Storytelling, by Rose McGee, describes the development and impact of Arts-Us Young Storytellers of Saint Paul, Minnesota.

Chapter 4: Voices of Students of All Ages

Liz Warren's **Creating Community through a College-Based Storytelling Program: The Storytelling Institute at South Mountain Community College** is an awe-inspiring look into how a college storytelling program expanded into the community and beyond.

In **Enriching Minds, Encouraging Hope and Joy: Columbus Story Adventures—a Community-Outreach Program of the Storytellers of Central Ohio**, Lyn Ford details a project that offers literacy skills and storytelling to students in at-risk situations, in summer programs that help them to maintain or improve their language-arts skills (reading, comprehension, speaking, and writing) levels for the next school year.

Taking the Stage: The Lone Star Student Storyteller Program is an ongoing project at the Frisco Public Library. This dedicated team of librarians provides detailed plans for creating a youth festival in your neck of the woods.

Nannette Watts describes the evolution and inner workings of **The National Youth Storytelling Showcase**, whose vision is "To empower the nation's youth through storytelling."

In **Heritage Night: School Programming**, Jane Stenson takes you step by step through the process of preparing children to research, write about, and tell stories of their families and community.

Chapter 5: Voices of the Disenfranchised

Lorna MacDonald Czarnota's **Crossroads: Stories for Reaching At-Risk Youth** describes her work developing a sense of trust, community, and safety among runaway teens by telling—and listening to—stories.

Pete and Joyce Vanderpool write lovingly about their inspiring work using the **Power of Creative Story for Alzheimer's Patients and Those with Other Special Needs**.

Gene and Peggy Helmick-Richardson provide us with an intimate glimpse into the challenges and rewards of **Storytelling in the Addiction Recovery Community**.

We heartily encourage you to identify a project that best suits your needs and *tweak* it! There will always be the need to adjust and modify in order to meet the needs of your own community and the resources available.

Go on, explore these model storytelling projects, get inspired, and then use these ideas as a catalyst for building community attachment, identity, and expression through storytelling! No two programs are alike, no two approaches are the same, but all of them speak to the heart through the magic of story.

Change the world—one person, one story, one community at a time.

Every great dream begins with a dreamer. Always remember, you have within you the strength, the patience, and the passion to reach for the stars to change the world.

—Harriet Tubman

Bibliography

Deedy, Carmen. "Foreword." In *Social Studies in the Storytelling Classroom: Exploring Our Cultural Voices and Perspectives*, edited by J. Stenson and S. Norfolk, 10. Little Rock, AR: Parkhurst Brothers, 2014.

Ganley, Barbara. "Re-Weaving the Community, Creating the Future: Storytelling at the Heart and Soul of Healthy Communities" (p. 6). Orton Family Foundation, 2010. https://www.orton.org/resources/storytelling_essay.

1

Voices for Intercultural Understanding

The history of storytelling isn't one of simply entertaining the masses but of also advising, instructing, challenging the status quo.

—Therese Fowler

Editors' Comments

Challenging the status quo—envisioning a world in which people see past "otherness" to the human being within: that is the hallmark of the projects described in this chapter. Each is animated by a deep belief in the power of storytelling to make that vision a reality.

Throughout these projects run central themes of passion, dedication, and hard work. The passion is evident: a passion for breaking down barriers of culture, ethnicity, and fear; a passion for helping people see each other as more alike than different; and a passion for kindling hope.

Dedication to success is palpable as well. There is a willingness—even an eagerness—to evaluate, assess, and adjust accordingly. "That's not how we've always done it" is not a maxim of this work. "How can we do it better?" is.

Another pervasive theme in these essays is teamwork—no one is in it alone. Each group internally forms a community and then presents itself to the world that joins in: another community!

Transforming Society through Youth Storytelling: Children at the Well

Paula Weiss

Every person alive on this wondrous planet is traveling solo between one ineffable mystery and another. We arise by miraculous means and are moment-to-moment contained, protected, and conveyed by our equally miraculous bodies and are preserved and presided over by the crowning achievements of evolution: our intellect, intuition, creativity, and transcendence. From the dawn of time, man has tried to make sense of it all. Is it any wonder that we reach out to others to form connections that orient and tether us to one another, our fellow travelers?

Joseph Campbell, American mythologist and storyteller, saw the individual's progression through life as essentially a hero's adventure, mostly initiated by recognition of the other. "When we quit thinking primarily about ourselves and our own self-preservation, we undergo a truly heroic transformation of consciousness."

It is through stories that we can "quit thinking primarily about ourselves" and learn to recognize the other. We tell stories to make meaning of our lives and to share our solitary reality. We listen carefully to stories of others to learn who they are and to get outside of ourselves. In all their vast array, stories are the essential catalysts and vehicles of Campbell's heroic transformation, of going beyond ourselves, and, therefore, of creating and transforming society.

The Children at the Well (C@W) storytelling program began in 2006 as an outgrowth of our local Interfaith Story Circle, founded in 1993 by Gert Johnson who became a cofounder and codirector of C@W. The intents of the youth program were to help young people tap into the richness of stories from their traditions to increase their understanding of and appreciation for diversity, to increase their empathy for others, and to enhance their self-discovery and development of voice.

The name of the program was inspired by Cherie Karo Schwartz's retelling of the biblical story of Isaac digging out his father Abraham's wells, which had been covered over. In the story, Isaac then significantly goes on to establish a new well that is indisputably his own, calling it "Rehovot"—"expansiveness." Israeli artist Yoram Raanan says of his painting drawn from this passage: "The Talmud teaches that water is an allusion to the Torah itself. The digging of wells is a search to reveal and spread its wellsprings" (http://www.yoramraanan.com/). To paraphrase Raanan, the wells can also be seen as a metaphor for the depths of our traditions, the depths inside each of us, and the search to find a more authentic and pure inner expression.

The C@W program encourages young people to explore the stories of their cultural, religious, and familial heritage as well as their own personal stories and gives them the tools and the opportunities to learn to tell those stories to audiences large and small. In addition, this program develops leadership and intercultural ambassadorship. It can be said that the ultimate goal of C@W is to harness the power of Campbell's heroic transformation in service to the transformation of society.

This is being written in the program's 10th year. Participants from the earliest years have blossomed into confident, empathetic, and flourishing young adults. We want to share our good fortune and our recipe for peace, understanding, and youth leadership. Instead of merely growing locally, we want to spread the seeds for this program. We are assembling a C@W Starter Kit to assist in starting similar programs, based closely or loosely on our model, according to your local needs and resources. Even if you are not ready for a full-blown program, we encourage you to try the pieces that are manageable for you. We are pleased to offer some of our "Kit" in this chapter: a bit of the program's history, management and funding considerations, and a glimpse inside some C@W moments, such as this, from longtime fan, storyteller Kate Dudding (www.katedudding.com):

> *What is most heartwarming to me and touches my soul is watching these young storytellers before and after the program. They group together, chattering away, gesturing dramatically, laughing often. All these young people from so many different cultures are now friends.*
>
> *One day, I was at a local story swap with three [of the] young men. Of course, they were sitting together. After several stories had been shared, there was a lull. The facilitator looked at them and said, "Does one of you have a story you'd like to share?"*
>
> *Ritam turned to Ben and said excitedly, "Tell them a Chelm story!"*
>
> *Khalafalla smiled and agreed, "Yes, tell them a Chelm story!"*
>
> *So Ben did, and we all laughed at the tale.*
>
> *I remember thinking: How many places in the world today would you find a Jew, a Hindu and a Muslim sitting down together as friends, and sharing stories?*
>
> *Then I thought, who would ever have imagined that one path to world peace goes directly through the village of Chelm?*

With funds from winning the National Storytelling Network's (NSN) Brimstone Award for 2005, C@W was launched by the Interfaith Story Circle, a group organized by Gert Johnson in 1993 around the compelling idea that sharing stories is a powerful way to connect people of different religions. In the years since, the mission of the Interfaith Story Circle has broadened to include connecting people of different cultures and philosophies as well as religions; it has also become involved in exciting local efforts to use stories to address economic and racial divides.

Similarly, C@W's focus has broadened. Somewhere along the way it was recognized that not all youngsters who get involved are of a particular religious tradition and that not all believe in a divine entity. This has been embraced as another form of diversity, and the addition of diverse voices to the mix has been welcome. It has been an important part of the program's growth.

What, then, are the essentials of C@W? Here is a list of basics; we feel so strongly about the fundamental importance of these elements that we ask storytelling programs modeling themselves on our template to adhere to these guidelines if they wish to use "Children at the Well" in their program's name.

- Participants are young and diverse, and they are taught the art of storytelling by a faculty that is equally diverse, gifted in working with young people, and skilled in storytelling and other spoken word performance arts.

- The group engages and learns about the group's diversity, mostly through stories.

- C@W story coaches employ appreciative coaching methods (see Marni Gillard's piece).

- Participants tell their own stories—from their lives, from their traditions, and from their heritage. The stories can be folktales, family stories, personal tales, or stories from scripture. While stories of cultures other than one's own can hold an exotic appeal and be tempting to use, and in fact are often told by other storytellers, in C@W it is felt that it is important to avoid cultural appropriation. An equally important reason to "dig stories from our own well" is for participants to deepen their connection to where they come from, for personal growth and development of voice.

- The C@W storytellers tell their stories from their imaginations, inspired by the feedback they get from their live audiences. They do not memorize, recite, or read their stories, though there have been some special exceptions to that.

- The program aspires to be intergenerational; the involvement of family members is sought after and welcomed through discussion groups, social gatherings, and volunteer opportunities. Family members are invited in to hear guest speakers, and they are encouraged to bring friends and family to performances. Their involvement supports, enriches, and magnifies the learning that their children are undertaking and grows community.

- While controversy is not shied away from, care is taken not to use stories that could cause harm by promoting stereotypes, by perpetuating damaging myths, or by denigrating a group of people. Some of the stories the participants tell are powerful statements of suffering and injustice; the stories speak for themselves.

Novelist Chimamanda Ngozi Adichie, in *The Danger of the Single Story*, a TED talk that has become widely circulated and influential, says:

Stories matter. Many stories matter. Stories have been used to dispossess and to malign, but stories can also be used to empower and to humanize. Stories can break the dignity of a people, but stories can also repair that broken dignity.

- Using Adichie's words, stories told at C@W are intended to empower, to humanize, and to repair.

A Glimpse into C@W: Light and Shadow

Demure, petite and ever-agreeable, Shadeh, 18, had been choosing to tell traditional tales that profess her strong belief in Islam, or were funny and lighthearted. But in her final year in Children at the Well, Shadeh decided to take a risk and create a story of the recent history of her father's beleaguered land; the Province of Nuristan, in Afghanistan. It was a story about war, terror and

*sudden death, but it was also about strong family ties and friend-
ships. It wasn't an easy project for one so sunny; she had to work
hard to find the right balance of light and shade to craft and tell
the story effectively.*

*As she told at the final performance, dressed in a striking blue
traditional costume, the audience was spellbound. Shadeh's mother
later reported that her husband had had tears in his eyes as he listened. Another audience member reported that learning Shadeh's
family history was "surprising and amazing." Shadeh herself
seemed to have grown in gravity and stature with the telling of the
story.*

Nuts and Bolts: Program Organization and Management

From the beginning, C@W has had a director (for the first several years,
codirectors) in addition to story coaches. Gert Johnson chose to structure the
program in this way, adding a layer of organizational complexity, which provides a strong team for vision setting, creative problem solving, and community outreach.

(Nuts First!); What Is the Director's Role?

- The director is responsible for all administrative tasks and is the primary dreamer behind program growth.
- She recruits students by organizing outreach events, building a data-
  base of contacts, corresponding with people and organizations
  throughout the year, keeping a waiting list of students, and soliciting
  letters of interest from potential students.
- She represents the program at conferences, events, and gatherings,
  sometimes with students and other staff.
- She recruits and hires coaches and assistants, with the involvement
  of the C@W program committee.
- She corresponds with parents and holds meetings with them.
- She gathers contact information, recruits volunteers, and manages
  their work.
- She meets with the coaches regularly during the C@W season and
  occasionally drops in on coaching sessions.
- With input from the coaches, she seeks out and schedules guest
  speakers and appearances of the C@W storytellers at community
  events, festivals, and conferences and arranges for enrichment workshops for the students and spaces for coaching, rehearsals, and
  performances.
- Most years, she, with the help of the C@W program committee, will
  make arrangements for a large final performance followed by mixer
  activities and (very popular!) international potluck suppers.
- She serves as program liaison to the board and, along with appropriate
  board committees, keeps track of finances, develops budgets, seeks and
  writes grants, organizes fund-raising events, and stewards donors.

- She publicizes C@W; she develops promotional material, takes and manages photos, and makes updates to the website and social media outlets.

Coaching Staff

The coaches are at the heart of C@W; it is of the highest priority to hire story coaches who are known for their exemplary work with young people, especially for their ability to encourage youngsters to flourish in their own way, without forcing a particular style on them. Being a good team player with an easygoing personality is high on the list and then comes professional experience with performing and storytelling skills. C@W coaches have been teachers, storytellers, spoken word artists, youth program directors, youth theater directors, librarians, or religious school educators. They all have had plenty of experience with performance.

It is equally important to seek out highly qualified young assistant coaches; they add a great deal of diverse talent, vitality, and perspective, and their presence ensures the program will be able to go on when the coaches leave or retire.

As with participants, it is important that coaches come from a variety of cultures and faith traditions.

The coaches meet together once before the year's coaching begins and weekly during the season. They attend all-staff meetings approximately once a month during that time and participate in a season wrap-up meeting after the final performances.

They meet with participants each Sunday afternoon for an average of four months and also may work with participants occasionally over the year. They have a direct, influential relationship with the students; they are highly effective in getting messages across to them (and their parents) about issues such as attendance, arriving on time, attending events such as our annual family picnic, and becoming involved in annual fund-raising events. It is part of their job responsibilities to assist with rallying the students to these causes, and it is essential to the program.

C@W coaches have developed their own curriculum, which is presented in full in our Starter Kit.

C@W Students

C@W students are gathered through various recruiting efforts from schools, places of worship, community centers, and elsewhere. Diversity is always being sought out. Teacher referrals have been very helpful in finding well-suited participants from families likely to be receptive. They range in age from 11 to 18; typically, they first join at ages 12–14.

Some may love to write stories, or have had experience with theater, but not most. Very important is that each student is genuinely interested in learning storytelling and in meeting others from a variety of backgrounds. The letter of interest that the director asks potential participants to write before being accepted is designed to elicit that information and make them aware of the commitment involved. Attendance is required; it is not a drop-in program. Ten to 20 students participate each year.

Enrichment

Guest speakers, workshops, and conversations with storytellers over Skype provide opportunities for participants to widen their experience with storytelling. It is important that the students meet people who use storytelling in their professions—not only professional storytellers—and hear about their work. Coaches stay for the presentations, introduce the guests, and participate. Parents and others are invited in to hear the guest speakers.

Guests from the communities represented by the students are especially sought; it is important for the students to see that their teachers, clergy, and other adult models have an honored place in the program, and it is important for them to meet mentors from the traditions of their fellow students.

Partnering

The NSN gave the program its start; at home, informal partnerships with area organizations and individuals have made it possible to build on that start. Many connections and friendships with clergy, teachers, community leaders, and people in the local media have been formed. Parents of C@W participants have been a wonderful source of ideas and support. Opportunities to connect with aligned programs, especially other youth programs, are always sought.

One ongoing fruitful involvement has been with the International Center of the Capital Region, which long ago began inviting C@W to meet with some of its international guests.

A Glimpse into C@W: Angels among Us

The International Center of the Capital Region sometimes invites Children at the Well *to meet with international delegations they host under the auspices of the State Department when they feel the interests of the visitors align with the program. It most often turns out to be a fascinating, warm exchange. But at times, that alignment of interests can feel a bit forced. This seemed to be the case at first when a group of C@W students, parents and staff were asked to meet with eight female scholars and teachers of Islamic law and religion from Jordan, and their interpreters. The women listened somewhat stonily as the* Children at the Well *program was explained to them and a story was told by one of the children. The interpreters accompanying them were kept busy throughout, perhaps adding to the consternation of the group. Questions they asked through the interpreters held challenges and belied doubt in the program's usefulness.*

Then 17-year-old Adah began to sing a beautiful lullaby while her father accompanied her on guitar. The song was "Angels' Blessing," written by Debbi Friedman, a composer of spiritual and accessible Jewish songs and melodies. The visitors continued to sit impassively and some of us began to wonder if we should have included this in the program. Perhaps the conservative religious values of the visitors were such that they disapproved of girls singing in mixed company — a possibility we should have but hadn't thought of ahead of time. If that was the case, it was too late at that point. But as the interpreters took a break and listened, we suddenly began to see smiles from the visitors. Something had caught their attention and approval. Our first thought was that it must have been that the song included very recognizable names of angels: Michael, Gavriel, Uriel, Rafael, revered also in Islam. We later pieced together that the song's refrain, a plaintive assurance that Shekinah (in Judaism, "a dwelling or settling of divine presence") was all around, had an almost identical counterpart in Islam. A cognate, sakïnah (in Arabic) signifies the "presence or peace of God." And here was this 17-year-old Jewish girl with the sweet voice singing a lovely song about concepts dear to their hearts. It was an "ah-ha!" moment; you could see the ice melt. The rest of the visit was quite cordial.

Also important have been connections made with organizations further afield. For us, this has included the Interfaith Youth Core; The Hickey Interfaith Center of Nazareth College (Rochester, New York); the TIDE Conference of YouthLead (Sharon, Massachusetts); the Brave New Voices Network of Youth Speaks; and an array of storytelling (and music) festivals.

C@W Story Coaching

The C@W coaches focus on building a strong community. During the first meeting, a pizza party is held and the coaches conduct ice-breaking and team-building exercises; the season's success depends on how well all bond at the beginning.

The C@W coaches believe in listening carefully to and learning from students. Many good ideas are incorporated into their teaching in the following way.

A Glimpse into C@W: Hero Worship

(From Nancy Marie Payne, C@W story coach; nancymariepayne. blogspot.com)

A new student had a very obvious case of Hero Worship for an older, more experienced teller. The older boy had a very distinctive style. Once, at the end of a session, well into the coaching season, we had some extra time. The staff asked the older boy to entertain the group with his story. The younger boy raised his hand and shyly asked if he could tell the older boy's story. The older student agreed. For the next 10 minutes the hero worshiper had us all in hysterics with his caricaturist imitation of his idol. When the laughing died down and eyes were wiped, the older student congratulated the younger one on his performance and said he had even learned a few techniques for his own telling. The staff has since incorporated the practice of sharing each other's stories into each training session.

Here are some other ways in which C@W story coaching may differ from the coaching in other youth storytelling programs.

- *Students are asked to choose stories that contain wisdom and are connected to their heritage.* Students and staff discuss the origins and significance of the stories chosen.

- *Students are encouraged not to sum up "The Moral" of any story in the telling,* as listeners receive the messages of stories in unique ways.
- *Storytelling ethics are taught and modeled.*
- *Each participant is given a journal* and asked to record their progress on a story, or what they want to improve, add to, or change.
- *Workshop sessions begin with a centering reflection or meditation* and often end with a reflection or prayer offered by a participant from their own tradition. The origins of the texts used are identified for educational purposes.
- *Vocal and physical exercises are a necessary part of every coaching session.*
- *Sensitivity to others is stressed in the choosing and telling of stories.*
- *Various options for finding stories are suggested.*
- *Snack breaks are weekly opportunities for socializing.*
- *Students are given the chance to work with all of the coaches* to experience the diversity of the coaching staff firsthand.

C@W storytellers and staff at the wonderful end-of-year performance and 10th-year anniversary celebration at First Unitarian Universalist Society of Albany, April 2015. Back row, left to right: Allison Lerman-Gluck (assistant coach), Nancy Marie Payne (coach), Abhinav Mehta, Ben Russell (coach), Rohan Ayachit, Danielle Charlestin (assistant coach), Samijo Buczeksmith, Kalyan Ramkumar, and Gert Johnson and Paula Weiss (cofounders and codirectors). Front row, left to right: Micki Groper (coach), Atharv Agashe, Shadeh Din, Varun Mondaiyka, Farriya Thalho, Sarah Davis, Ayah Osman, Riane Richard, and Marni Gillard (former coach). Not pictured: Peter Meshkov.

Macaela Rourke and Salamatu Mohammed work on their stories at the Colonie Town Library, 2011. Salamatu, from Ghana, was spending a year as an exchange student with another participant's family in Salem, New York. Macaela's family later hosted an exchange student (from Armenia) who joined C@W in 2013; lucky for us, in both cases!

- *C@W tellers are coached to be ambassadors of peace and understanding through storytelling* as well as strong tellers.

A central tenet of C@W coaching is that successful experiences build confidence. Students are guided to choose stories within their reach to learn, and they are taught how to modify their stories for successful telling.

Leading with positive comments in all interactions is emphasized, particularly when giving feedback to tellers as they rehearse their stories.

Following is an excerpt from the Starter Kit showing the underlying approach to C@W story coaching that Marni Gillard and Mary Murphy were instrumental in developing.

Coaching Tellers to Be Their Unique Selves (by Marni Gillard; marnigillard.com)

> *... The coach uses his or her intelligence to awaken the creative intelligence of the burgeoning artist. As the old saying suggests, "Teach them to fish and you feed them for a lifetime." Ideas below adapted from the writings and workshops of Doug Lipman.*
>   *http://storydynamics.com/*
>   *https://www.facebook.com/douglipman*

Farriya "cracks right up" at something Rohan has said . . . while waiting in line at the postperformance potluck, April 2015.

1. ***BELIEVE*** *in every teller's potential. Commit to watching for and focusing on a teller's natural strengths. Believe in the artistry ready to be awakened. Success is unique to every teller.*

2. ***LISTEN*** *from a relaxed, valuing stance. A listening coach doesn't interrupt nor give suggestions when a tale is new. Advice has its place eventually, but growth begins with delighted receiving. "You did that! Well done!" quiets anxiety and builds the desire to improve.*

3. ***APPRECIATE*** *specifically and globally. Coaches and peer listeners notice and share what worked. Specific appreciations: word-choice, tone, pace, gesture, surprises or anything satisfying. Specific appreciations alert all who are listening to the countless hows of successful storytelling. "Great pause there—you gave us time to imagine." "That moment (phrase, facial expression, movement) grabbed me!" "That was an authentic mom tone of voice!" "Cool sound effect . . ."*

Where are coaching meetings held? The program does not yet have its own space; meetings have been held mostly in donated spaces; at homes, public libraries, at schools and at places of worship.

The weekly meeting place needs to be centrally located, with easy enough access by foot and by car. It must have a large space for the entire group, including an area for some limited physical exercise, as well as room for small groups to work simultaneously without being a distraction to each other. Finally, it's important that they allow food, so that snacks can be brought in!

On our way from Albany to the United Nations to attend a "High-Level Meeting" and participate in interfaith dialog to commemorate the International Year of Youth, July 22, 2011. The hottest day of the year ... all five immediately scrambled to the top and back of the (thankfully very well air-conditioned) MegaBus so they could sit together in a row!

Left to right: Kartik Ramkumar, Sarah Syed, Emily Hebert, Aditya Agashe, and Alaudeen Umar.

Funding

In order to seek donations and grants to sustain the program, we quickly realized we would need to find a fiscal sponsor, partner with an established group, or form a nonprofit and then gain tax exempt status. No tuition was charged for the first five years of the program, but it gradually became clear that funders appreciate knowing a program is making an attempt to be self-sustaining. It was decided to charge a modest tuition while letting it be known that tuition would be waived for participants whose families were not able to pay.

Starter Kit

Now that you have learned about C@W, are you considering starting a storytelling program like ours? First, spend time assessing your own community's needs. Are there divides you would want to try to address with storytelling? How would you want your own youth storytelling program to build bridges and make a difference in your community?

Then, consider your resources. Where and how would you find your staff and storytellers? Who would be the program's allies? What are the community organizations, schools, and places of worship that you could connect

Audience members watching the storytelling April 25, 2015.

with? What are the distant organizations that could support the program in various ways? Remember, if you are not ready to take on the full program, try a piece.

The C@W Starter Kit will be available soon. Please contact us at directorcaw@gmail.com or through childrenatthewell.org if you would like to discuss the possibilities. We would love to hear from you!

Social Justice Storytelling Then and Now

Susan O'Halloran

Talking about controversial subjects can easily become argumentative debates where people feel even more locked into their opposing positions. It makes most of us want to avoid "difficult" subjects such as race, class, gender, sexual orientation, physical abilities, and the like altogether. How do we lessen what divides us? How do we listen to another person or group's perspective respectfully?

I am more convinced than ever that storytelling gives us one of the best ways to talk about potentially divisive topics. It is hard to argue with someone else's personal and emotional experiences. Stories give us a compassionate way to interact by moving us from argument to dialogue, from a debate-team mentality ("I'm right; you're wrong") to the language of the heart ("You and I are connected").

Since 1996, I have partnered with Father Derek Simons who runs a communications ministry through his religious order, the Society of The Divine Word. I remember him approaching me at the 1995 Illinois Storytelling Festival and asking, "How do you get so much meaning into your stories?" We met soon after and realized we shared a common vision of using storytelling to promote understanding and reconciliation around issues of difference in our community, especially around race. Our collaboration has led us into 20 years of community-based live, online, and media-driven storytelling projects.

Multicultural Live Performances

In our first partnership, we coproduced a live performance piece called "Tribes & Bridges" (with Antonio Sacre who is Cuban and Irish American and La'Ron Williams who is African American and myself an Irish American teller). In our show, Antonio shared the hurdles of growing up a "Leprecano." He auditioned for theater roles, for example, only to discover that he was too white for some casting directors and too "ethnic" for others. La'Ron described a nurturing, third-grade teacher taking the brown crayon out of his hand when he wanted to color the people he had just drawn and, without a word, handing him, instead, the (peach-colored) crayon marked, "Flesh." I told about observing my first civil rights demonstration in high school in segregated Chicago and feeling the wrenching of my spirit as I stood by helplessly watching two African American women who had befriended me being hauled away by the police. I knew I could not actively support these women in their all black community, nor could I even speak of witnessing their heroism when I returned to my all white neighborhood.

We performed this show in church basements, in high school auditoriums with a thousand students on bleachers, and even on the stage of Chicago's esteemed Steppenwolf Theatre. In April 2001, I had the honor of being part of the press conference for the cardinal archbishop of Chicago who was releasing a pastoral letter on racism. I performed an excerpt of one of my social justice stories to the Chicago media right before the cardinal made his presentation.

Whether in front of the media's bright lights or before a classroom of students, or in the pain and joys of an antiracism retreat for adults, we heard over and over again, "I didn't know (fill in the blank about someone else's culture and history) . . ." and "That was my story, too!" We knew we were on to something.

A Social Justice Storytelling Festival

We wanted to give these kinds of stories a larger setting. In 2003, we decided to create a three-day festival focusing on social justice stories, especially racial justice stories that could be tough as well as entertaining. The JustStories Festival took a variety of shapes over its nine-year run, but four key components remained throughout:

1. A fellowship award—Storytellers *had* social justice stories; they were living their lives in twentieth-century America. However, for those making their living telling stories, their time was better spent learning the folktales or creating humorous personal stories that producers were requesting. Father Derek Simons through his communications ministry was able to offer tellers the financial support to give time to and focus on developing more culturally challenging stories as well as a place to perform them at our JustStories Festival.

2. Always more than one—Most story festivals in trying to be diverse and inclusive will hire one African American teller, one Asian American, one person from a First Nation, and so forth. Unless it is a huge national festival that showcases 20-some tellers, most festivals are restricted to 4–6 tellers. Besides the fact that tellers from a particular cultural heritage rarely have the opportunity to perform together, an additional unintended consequence of the "one of each" approach is that some in the audience may expect the teller to be speaking for his or her group. JustStories was a small festival as well, but rather than showcasing one teller from each group, we committed to presenting fewer groups and including 2–3 tellers from any cultural background, or, in some cases such as our *Asian Voices* Festival, having all of our tellers from one heritage so the audience could experience the variety of thoughts and experiences within a culture.

3. Give equal time to audience participation—So often after we storytellers perform, people come up to us and tell us their stories. We say that we tell stories in part to help other people remember and tell theirs, but then we do not provide a format to do so. We designed a festival with longer sessions so that audience reflection was built in from simple question and answer periods to having the audience share *their* stories in partners or small groups and then with the larger audience. Throughout the day, we also included time slots that were not storytelling per se but a chance to discuss the issues the stories were bringing up. For example, representatives from various community groups such as ASE, the Chicago-based part of the National Association of Black Storytellers, or the Christian-Muslim dialogue group led discussions and informed people of the community resources and actions. We also included whole time slots devoted to interactive exercises that I might include in one of my Diversity and Inclusion seminars such as a fishbowl exercise where different racial groups can be flies on the wall listening in as another group discusses the questions and topics the audience most wanted to hear.

4. Engaging storytelling—Storytelling was at the center of all our presentations and breakout sessions. Even when we held sessions

featuring community members, not professional tellers, such as the Arab or Muslim panel or the Vietnamese American performance, the tellers and presenters used humor and all the engaging tools of the art form to keep our social justice stories and discussions from deteriorating into polemics and diatribe.

Videotaping Community Stories of Discrimination and Triumphs

During this same time period, Father Derek and I were busy supporting the content for a teen social justice group in the Archdiocese of Chicago. To provide us with graphic posters, programs, and the like, I introduced Father Derek to Kris Evenson of CaptureHits Marketing Group (www. CaptureHits.com).

Teachers accompanied their students to the monthly gatherings and began to clamor for most of the kinds of exercises we were offering the teens. From that request, I developed a two-year high school diversity curriculum, Kaleidoscope: Valuing Differences and Creating Inclusion. Because Father Derek had been involved in radio and TV for many years and I had worked as a producer and writer for video companies, we decided to include a video component to the curriculum.

Most of our schools' staff are predominantly white and female and on their own do not look like the world in which many of our students are and will be living. However, it is challenging for teachers to get busy community people to come into a school to talk to and work with students. We decided to bring a diverse array of adults and high school students into the classrooms via videotapes. I interviewed over 70 people to find 40, whose stories fit with the lesson plans in the Kaleidoscope curriculum.

In these videos, the students hear a grown woman talk about the ethnic slurs she heard on the grammar school playground and then watch her well up with tears, the sting of humiliation still raw in her soul 30 years later. In another interview, we listen to the story of a young woman who had only two sets of clothes as a young girl. She would wash one set in the bathtub each night but, sometimes, the clothes would not dry. She would be forced to wear the same outfit to school two days in a row. Her classmates' teasing was relentless.

Another young woman who is Native American describes watching her classmates jump about the classroom with whoops and screams thinking they were doing some kind of authentic American Indian dance. She listened to her teacher describe the First Nations of this country as "uncivilized." She speaks about how few of us learn in our current school systems about America as a nation with many sovereign nations within it. "Without this education," she asks, "how are people to make sense out of different rules or laws for one group of people in contrast to another? No wonder we have fights over things such as land and hunting rights."

With simple sharing, we were able to tell the stories of people who have been designated as outsiders in our country and, at the same time, make the invisible lessons and privileges of the insiders more visible. Telling stories of exclusion as well as the great sacrifices people have made toward inclusion lets students know that they have a part to play. They can be actors making a difference.

The Kaleidoscope curriculum and videos were distributed to 47 Catholic high schools in Chicago and to other schools as well. We began to experience the power of using media to reach a larger audience.

Videotaping Professional Tellers' Social Justice Stories

From these community-based videos, it was an easy leap to start video-taping professional storytellers telling their life stories of barriers faced and overcome. We started with videotaping the tellers who we were flying into Chicago for our JustStories Festivals. Kris Evenson who had been our graphic designer for the teen social justice club was and is, in addition, an ace web designer and marketer. With Father Derek's support, Kris created a website (now called www.RacebridgesStudio.com) for these professional storytellers' videos as well as free downloads of lesson plans and articles for teachers and other community groups wanting to talk about race.

It took us awhile to find our style. Eventually, we landed on shooting the tellers in a simple, straight-on, head-and-shoulders format. We were after the feeling of intimacy, the feeling that the teller was sitting across the kitchen table from you, the viewer. We also asked the tellers to keep going if there was a "mistake" just as they would during a live performance. This also helped the video to feel like a spontaneous conversation.

We began to expand our videotaping to include other local and national storytellers who had these types of stories. We flew them into Chicago and eventually and more cost-effectively shot the videotapes at the NSN's conferences where hundreds of tellers were already gathered.

For the tellers, this kind of production is more akin to creating a story for a radio program. Each teller owns his or her story and performance (in exchange for letting us record them, each teller was given a digital version of his or her story that he or she could use elsewhere such as on his or her own websites or burn onto DVDs and the benefit of being on our site and YouTube channel). I worked with the tellers to create a written version of each story weeks and even months before the video shoot. When you are paying a professional crew thousands of dollars and working on a tight schedule, you cannot take the time to tweak a story on location.

An Online Storytelling Festival

In 2011, we held our last live JustStories Festival and, then, turned our attention to the RaceBridges Studio website sponsored by Derek Simons's Angels Studio. Facebook was well established by this time having moved from college campuses to the general public in 2005. I think Derek, Kris, and I were all noodling around on the web when the idea struck: What if we put our videos on someone else's Internet platform where people already are, rather than always striving to drive people in one direction to our site?

Friends Invite Friends

Nothing takes the place of live storytelling, but an *online* storytelling festival held the possibility of being even more far-reaching than a live event ever could be. On an established platform such as Facebook, once someone became a "fan" of our videos, all their friends saw the videos, too. People, through their interest, would do much of the marketing for us.

Most importantly, on Facebook, the software was already built in for people to comment on posts. No more expensive costs for a comment board for your community. We watched people commenting on each other's posts and thought: "Wow, if we showed our videos on Facebook, the audience could comment. The storyteller could be online live and immediately respond to questions—just like a live question and answer session after a performance.

We can have a worldwide conversation on race with stories as the center-piece!" The first ever online storytelling festival was born!

We decided to hold the Festival in 2012 for three days to give it a large presence—a new storyteller telling multiple stories every half an hour from 8 a.m. to midnight.

Marketing

We started the JustStories Facebook page in February 2012 to build our fan base. We knew we could not announce an August festival in August and expect people to pay attention. As each person "liked" our page, our posts went into their "feed" and their friends saw the posts and could share them as well. In the months leading up to the festival, we ran pre-views of some of the videos, shared resources, talked about current diver-sity issues, and kept asking over and over again for people to share our posts and to "like" our page.

Additionally, we ran NSN ads online and in *Storytelling Magazine* along with passing out fliers and bookmarks at the July NSN Conference. Plus, we used Facebook ads and every other social media outlet: Twitter, LinkedIn, and Pinterest. We offered nonprofits, other storytelling festivals, and the sto-rytellers themselves prizes and online mentions during the festival for send-ing our promotional materials to their e-mail lists and highlighting us in *their* social media.

Talking to the World in My Home Office

And, then, we went live! I wish I had had someone videotaping me as the festival went live. The scene was hysterical. I sat alone in my office talking to the world. I was tied to my computer for 16 hours a day. I was enlarging each video to full screen on schedule, monitoring comments, calling the next teller to make sure they were online, troubleshooting technical snafus, responding to instant messages, commenting on the stories and audience's questions, sharing related resources, and so on. I ate lunch, watered my plants, and brushed my teeth, with my laptop in the crook of my arm and my phone in my other hand.

Challenges

Throughout the lead-up to the festival and even during the festival, I fielded complaints from irate storytellers who found the whole idea of an on-line festival deplorable, but the great majority of challenges during the actual online festival had to do with technology. It is hard to remember that even a few short years ago, Facebook and other similar platforms were new to many people. During the festival, I had storytellers call me in a panic because they could not get into their account or they swore they were answering people's questions but did not see their responses on the site. I had audience members calling me, too, such as the concierge from an assisted living apartment tell-ing me that a 97-year-old resident wanted to watch the festival but could not find it.

Favorite Moments

But I feel that the stories themselves were worth the fight with technol-ogy and made believers out of many storytelling fans. Even though Derek and

I recorded every one of those stories, and Kris and I edited the videos to remove background sounds and to add introductions and credits (which meant watching them over and over again), I was still moved by watching them all together over the three full days of the festival.

I remember one exchange after Jane Stenson and Jo Radner's stories were shown. Both women told about discovering that their great-grandfathers had been involved in the genocide of First Nations' people. Several people from different First Nations wrote in talking about how to turn guilt and shame into something productive. Then, a man from Germany wrote saying he had discovered that his father was a Nazi. As audience members exchanged support and advice, they were helping each other to reconcile their feelings about the positive and terrible truths of their families' and country's histories. And, now, they had a whole set of stories in common with which to reference their feelings. International healing was occurring over the Internet!

The festival also helped our tellers to feel connected. Family, friends, and colleagues who had never seen a teller perform now had the chance, and many tellers heard from relatives who had never heard a particular family story and were so very grateful. One of our tellers, Arif Choudhury, was traveling when his stories ran—so he was answering people's questions while riding in the backseat of a car in rural Bangladesh. I had always imagined somebody in Mississippi talking to somebody in Australia, talking to somebody in New York, or talking to somebody in Brazil, and that was just what happened. Plus, a number of shut-ins from around the world wrote to tell me that it was the first time they were able to attend a storytelling festival in years.

Statistics Told a Story

Most of our audience was from the United States, but we also had listeners/participants from Canada, the United Kingdom, Australia, Germany, New Zealand, Israel, Brazil, India, Spain, Switzerland, Greece, Ireland, Philippines, Sweden, Argentina, Russia, Taiwan, Norway, and Italy. By the second year of the online festival in 2013 (then called Stories Connect Us All), we had reached 52 countries.

We had a "Facebook reach" of 51,000 the first year and 112,000 the second year. The industry standard for going viral (meaning people engage with the online content by commenting, liking, or sharing a post, etc.) states that anything above a 1.9 percent response rate is outstanding; the average *virality* of our posts was 2.47 percent.

With participants helping us to market the festival, we reached people far beyond the typical storytelling audience. For example, one of our largest audiences was 25–34-year-old males! In the second year, we also had more people participate in groups such as people watching together at libraries and in classrooms or streaming at college student centers.

While I was pleased that no haters joined in (not one racist comment during either festival), I did miss the amount of discussion and learning that took place during our live JustStories Festivals. The majority of written comments were about how great the stories were—which was nice—but, if I were to do the festival again, I would have multiperson panel discussions, live streaming keynotes, and question and answer sessions *on the topics* on which the stories touched. With advancements in technology, even more is possible than when we first produced the online storytelling festival in 2012. But, for now, you can view for free the 160+ stories we have videotaped over the years by going to www.RacebridgesStudio.com.

Challenging but Worth It

If you are going to perform or produce stories around race and issues of justice, be prepared for deep emotions to arise, yours and others. All good outer work starts with the inner. Before attempting live or online storytelling events in the community that focus on social issues, understand your relationship to the subject. Get to know your hiding places, your large cache of prejudices and fears. Cozy up to your shadow side or else you will sound righteous and people will close down. Take the responsibility to educate yourself. People who have been placed on the outside in our society have enough burdens without feeling as though they are specimens under a microscope or spokespersons for their entire group and they are there to enlighten you.

Plus, when presenting our country's hidden history around race, for example, we must be careful not to paint any group as victim only but to always include the magnificent stories of resistance and success and everyday happiness as well.

Throughout, be a compassionate colleague. As you collaborate and discuss the care and nurturing of your audiences, you must do the same for each other. Our hurts run deep. Tears will be shed; memories and, therefore, creation will be blocked; and doubts will continually make themselves known. We have to have a long and large love for our stories, our country, and each other to keep going. If you are hitting the true repressed veins of our individual and communal psyches, I would imagine your team will experience some of the things we have: fitful sleep, times of "I can't do this," and moments of incredible connection and freedom as we finally faced and spoke long-buried truths. Community storytelling can inspire us to see ourselves and our country as mosaics of strength, strong enough and large enough to hold everybody's story.

Multicultural Family Adventures in Reading

Onawumi Jean Moss

In 2008, I had the good fortune to be one of four local storytellers selected to help launch the Family Adventures in Reading (FAIR) program: "a humanities-based project tailored to the needs of neighborhoods in Springfield, Massachusetts." The Springfield City Library system, with the support of three community-based service agencies, served as host. The primary goal of the FAIR program was to involve children, their parents, and caregivers in reading, learning, and expressing opinions about award-winning books (K-8).

Storytellers and texts were selected based on their well-known capacity to:

a. draw multicultural audiences into entertaining and educative experiences;
b. show respect for the role of these intended families—mainly African American, Latino, and Mexican—as desirable community assets; and
c. encourage lasting, action-oriented connections between families and the library.

Engaging Families in an Entertaining, Educative Multicultural Experience

Ready! Set! Go! Doors open, the clock is running; I have 90 minutes to be a culturally aware and flawless entertainer with riveting discussion skills to die for. Oh, fly away butterflies ... fly away. Good—I am ready for my close-up.

WELCOME! WELCOME! WELCOME! The assigned meeting room is relatively small; I choose to stand near the center. Participants heard "WELCOME so glad you could come." I respectfully decline the temptation to welcome in Spanish. I inquire, and my library host informs me of a grandparent who speaks very little English; her granddaughter is her interpreter. I apologize for not knowing how to speak Spanish; she forgives me. Everybody laughs; that is an unexpected bonus. WHY? I am sure there are many number of reasons for the jovial reactions. Here is mine: in that moment, the deference I paid to the only elder in the room showed appropriate cultural civility.

Here is a snapshot of how I prepared. Being southern born and bred, I was taught to treat everyone the way I would want them to treat me. In the course of working with students and adults of various backgrounds, everything I was taught has been reinforced and elevated.

Courtesy, respect, and trust are revered building blocks of cultures throughout the world; recognition of an individual's dignity is an integral part of that triad. With that in mind, I focused on developing profiles of my assigned communities using information gleaned from the orientation session along with responses to my interviews of friends and colleagues from similar cultural backgrounds. By all accounts, the greatest risk being invented or unique names, it made sense to use names and proverbs (wise old sayings) as an educative and entertaining means of fostering a sense of group connection.

I started by saying: Onawumi means "one who is creative and loves to create," Jean means "gift of God," and Moss connects me with my children. I chose this proverb: "Your name," according to the Yoruba of Nigeria, "gives you presence, beauty and power."

Since everyone was told what to expect upon arrival, those who needed to had made good use of their phones. In a few moments, most of them were able to share embellished meanings of their names as well as fond memories of how and why they recalled wise old sayings. Humorous one-minute stories showed up. Early on, I coached the middle-school student, a girl who was somewhat unsure about what to say. Once she had access to positive descriptors, she took charge. YES! Throughout the opening I sang "Hello How Do You Do?" At intervals each person's name was repeated in unison by the entire group. We closed by answering "Fine, thank you!" The aim of this deeply personal activity was to give participants an opportunity to speak freely and respectfully of themselves. FANTASTIC! The abandonment of sweeping generalities is crucial to developing mutual respect in multicultural settings. This is one of the countless ways to begin achieving such a desirable outcome.

We had no difficulty being hands-on with the next task of READING ALOUD masterfully.

Read Aloud, Talk Back, and Reference Displays

The READ ALOUD was designed to inspire the practice of reading as an enjoyable, thought-provoking, and animated family-friendly social activity.

This storyteller/coach begins with a brief discussion of the author, title, and illustrations followed by an animated overview of the story.

Having willing group members work on being narrators (readers) and others to play characters (performers) during a 5–10 minute rehearsal, coached by family members and with help from the roving S/C (that is me) available upon request, sets a community engagement off. Narrators and characters were encouraged to be expressive and to feel free to call time out at anytime they feel it necessary to do so. Such a request usually means they have grown self-conscience for one reason or another. Whatever the reason, this S/C invites the group to join in giving high fives coupled with WAY TO GO and BIG THANK YOU! Time permitting, we move ahead.

The TALK-BACK discussion focuses on themes of courage, determination, fairness, and so on, with emphasis on having a noncompetitive conversation versus debating the pros and cons of the featured text. This S/C suggests asking students reflective questions that draw them into the story: "How did this story make you feel about being _____ [insert theme]?"

On the other hand, parents might be better served by responding to more interpretive questions: "In talking with your family about _____ [conversation], in what ways might this story influence that?"

The REFERENCE DISPLAYS were an exclusive feature of my sessions. At my request, materials were exhibited on library carts to place greater emphasis on the vast, yet manageable resource known as the library. These exhibits consisted of (a) dictionaries and Thesaurus; (b) biographies (author and illustrator); (c) maps to establish noted geographical settings, for example, Zimbabwe; and (d) *Mufaro's Beautiful Daughters* and other books and publications by the featured author. This feature received high praise and brisk patronage of the Children's Room.

Although minimal staffing resulted in discontinuance, the point was to help students and parents develop stronger bonds within their community and with their library. It worked!

Building International Community through Storytelling

Dr. Aaron Wills and Dr. Lisa Overholser with Sherry Norfolk

The Background in a Nutshell (Sherry Norfolk)

"Bobby, Sherry, I want to send Taiwanese students to the United States to be in a storytelling festival. Can you help me?"

My husband and I were sitting in a restaurant in Taichung, Taiwan, with Joey Wong, the president of MMC Starlight GRC, as she explained her vision.

"You see, we have student storytellers ages 8 through 14 who are learning to tell stories in English to English-speaking audiences. I want them to participate in an American storytelling festival and also to attend a typical American school for several days and to homestay with typical American families. They will share insights about Taiwanese culture and learn about American culture. They will be motivated to speak and learn more English language. How can we make this happen?"

We discussed possible scenarios and provided links to the websites of the American storytelling festivals, which are known to feature student tellers as well as professional tellers. Joey studied the various models and determined that the St. Louis Storytelling Festival seemed to best meet her needs.

Bobby and I are on the St. Louis Storytelling Festival Advisory Committee, so we agreed to bring her proposal to the attention of the committee. We also agreed to identify a school that would be interested in hosting the youth tellers in the classrooms and to provide homestay families.

Back home in St. Louis, we presented the idea to the committee, and upon its approval, began liaising between Starlight, the executive director of the St. Louis Storytelling Festival, and the festival sponsor, University of Missouri Extension, to develop an agreement and issue letters of invitation and a memorandum of understanding (MOU) between the university, the festival, and Starlight.

With that in the works, we identified a school that would not just allow but also *welcome* the Starlight Ambassadors. We approached Dr. Aaron Wills, principal of Claymont Elementary in the Parkway School District, and upon his enthusiastic response ("That would be great for the kids!"), we met with him and the Parent Teacher Organization (PTO) president.

We were very fortunate to find the right welcoming, enthusiastic school—*top priority!*—and begin working with them early enough to give them time to do all of this background work. It takes a *lot of time* for the administrative details, for the families to be chosen, and for logistics to be worked out.

Back in Taiwan, Joey was screening and training the ambassadors. She began by requesting a formal recommendation from the school principal for the kids who wished to join the team, covering each student's general classroom performance not just in school work but as a team player as well. Next, there was an audition, during which the students had to tell their favorite tale or share an incident they can never forget in their lives. They also had to tell Joey why they wanted to join the Starlight program and what they knew about being a "goodwill ambassador." Based on the above, she made assessments and started filtering through the heaps of applicants.

Meanwhile, Dr. Lisa Overholser, the director of the St. Louis Storytelling Festival, was determining appropriate venues and schedules for the Starlight Goodwill Ambassadors. In the first year, that meant scheduling 28 kids; the second year, there were 42! The stories were short—only three minutes—but that was still a lot of storytelling to schedule and logistics to juggle! Lisa also worked within the university to create the MOU and to provide an appropriate signing ceremony and gift exchange.

That is the background, in a nutshell. The best people to discuss the program from each distinct perspective, however, are the main players themselves: Joey Wong, Lisa Overholser, and Aaron Wills. I now turn the podium over to them.

Joey Wong, MMC Starlight GRC

In the *2016 US Tour Report,* Joey Wong explained the concept of the Starlight Goodwill Ambassadors and the outcomes of the program:

> *The inception of the Starlight Goodwill Ambassador Educational and Cultural Program took place in 2014. This program is owned jointly by MMC Starlight Group of companies and Starlight Education Foundation. The core value of this program is to enhance the ability of Taiwan students to interact with people around the world in English thereby elevating their future international competitive edge. The aim is to promote Taiwan and the Chinese culture / history. The delivery method is by way of storytelling!*
>
> *Through the Starlight Goodwill Ambassador program, the students who are selected through a critical screening test get the*

Starlight Goodwill Ambassadors make lifelong friends with their homestay families.

Starlight Goodwill Ambassadors make lifelong friends with their homestay families.

opportunity to travel as a team to many countries in the world, gaining significant knowledge during each journey. They are all given a specific mission—to spread goodwill amongst their own team members, in the foreign schools where they gain a short term collaborative learning experience, in the home families where they stay during the travel and, to the audience of the festivals or events they attend during the travel. Starlight Goodwill Ambassadors go through a whole six months of storytelling and etiquette training by our teachers before they actually travel overseas. The stories selected are aimed at promoting Taiwan from a cultural and tourism viewpoint or otherwise sharing interesting Chinese folktales and myths.

The young ambassadors are always accompanied by our team leaders and foundation board members during each travel to ensure safety and care giving. Many school principals and parents often join the trip to enjoy the students' performance and also to explore the differences in the overseas school environment and teaching methodology. They also visit the homestay families to share gifts from Taiwan and to thank the home parents for taking great care of our goodwill ambassador students.

At the end of each program when the students return to Taiwan, they will be requested to present their travel experience in their schools and to write a short memoir. The Starlight Goodwill Ambassadors always return with full interaction confidence,

Starlight Goodwill Ambassadors make lifelong friends with their homestay families.

gaining an extensive independence and with a monumental desire to further improve their English communication skills, in anticipation of the next trip!

Some of those (unedited) memoirs follow:
健行國小 王昱喬 (Joanne):

I'm so glad that I have the honor to attend 2015 Starlight good will ambassadors the US tour, I learned a lot during these 11 days. I not only had my very first trip to the US, but also learned about American's life. Our homestay family was so nice to us, they gave me not only shelter, but also love. They even gave me gifts although it was free.

Claymont was the second best part. Doctor Wills, the principal of claymont, was really ardour. The kids there were cute and kind too! They even gave me cards, and I felt so sweet. I am really happy and I'm looking forward to the next trip.

大墩國小 黃偉綸 (Matthew):

I am very honored to have the chance to attend the 2015 US Starlight Goodwill Ambassadors.

Even though it was not my first time in the US, I have still learned lots of things during these 11 days including American life-style, history and different culture.

I also liked Claymont Elementary, because everybody there welcomed us with open hands, especially Principal Wills and the students in my class. On the last day they gave us "Goodbye" cards, this touched me greatly.

I absolutely loved my homestay family (the DeLuca family) because they were so nice and also, when my roommate Jacky and I didn't know how to speak the word in English, they were patient and gave us time to speak. When my phone broke down, my home-mom and homedad went out of their way to help me get it fixed, and during the time my phone was being fixed they even lent me their camera!!! They were so kind. When they gave me a photo album with photos of the times we spent with them, it touched me so much I almost cried. I miss my homefamily very much! I hope one day that they can visit us.

I will always remember this trip and I look forward to the next one.

清水國小 張詠馨 (Madeline):

This is my first time to go to the USA, I felt so excited.

I went to St. Louis to attend St. Louis Story Telling Festival. All of the group members told our stories in libraries, communities, and schools. It's a very special expereince that I could tell a story in a foreign country. Besides, we had homestay opportunities to be hosted in host families. The group member, Selina, and I were hosted in Spillman family. There were three dauthers, two cats, and a dog in my host family. Auntie Mary, Ms. Spillman, prepared breakfast and took us to school everyday. After school, she often prepared icecream for us. We had a good time there. When we've gone to leave the USA, my host family gave me a lot of gifts, cookies, caps, dolls, T-shirts, etc. They were really nice to me, and I missed them so much.

I learned story telling skills, experienced different life and made some good friends. If you ask me how do I feel about this activity? My answer is it's fantastic! I love it!!

明道中學 魏學楹 (Amanda):

This is definitely an unforgettable trip!

This tour first caught my eye for the chance of learning storytelling, which is one of my best hobbies. Then I realized that we will be living with our host families during our stay in St. Louis. That was so exciting to know, because I had always dreamed to have an experience like that. This made a perfect match for me—storytelling and home stay experience, so it would be a pity if I didn't go. When the bus was pulling onto the front of Claymont Elementary, I could hear the cheering of the kids, and then I saw a group of jovial people welcoming us. It was absolutely the best part. We were sent home to our own families after the greetings, and started our "new" life. It was a lot of fun to be eating American foods, going to American schools, and enjoying American lives. I was so excited when I got my lunch box—a brown paper bag, which Americans usually say: "I'm brown-bagging it." I went to the school and had some classes with the kids. Lastly, the storytelling began, and we all performed on the stage. Those were really great opportunities to get to speak in public. The last day of storytelling, we attended the closing ceremony, and saw lots of amazing storytellers who came to perform. I learned a lot from them. Through this trip, there were so many people to thank and so many friends to remember.

I'm still in contact with my host families, they are just so sweet!

I went deep into Americans lives through this experience, and made a good ambassador. I hope that the Americans have made a good impression on us!

Lisa Overholser, University of Missouri Extension

Storytelling is a timeless, universal art form. Stories serve as an intuitive, intrinsic way to pass on history and knowledge from person to person and from one generation to another. They shape cultural values and cultural knowledge and are a powerful method of learning. Told in the oral tradition long before they were written down, the telling of stories has also long relied on communicative skill and competence.

The St. Louis Storytelling Festival, an annual, multiday event typically held the first weekend of May, celebrates this art form with performances, workshops, and special storytelling events all across the St. Louis metropolitan region. Started in 1980 by the College of Arts and Sciences' Continuing Education Department of the University of Missouri–St. Louis, the Festival was held on the grounds of the St. Louis Gateway Arch, an iconic, historic symbol, in a collaborative effort that was meant to enliven St. Louis's history by putting a dynamic, "living" voice to it. It shone a spotlight on the living history of St. Louis at that time by highlighting stories and storytellers important in St. Louis's historical development, at the same time that professional storytelling was blossoming.

In its 37 years, the Festival's commitment to community outreach and collaboration became further strengthened in 2014 when the University of Missouri Extension's Community Arts Program became the Festival's new partner. While still a part of the statewide University of Missouri system, the mission of Extension is to enrich the lives of Missouri's citizens by engaging with people and communities to understand change, solve problems, and make informed decisions. The Extension's Community Arts Program does this through arts-based economic and community development. That is a powerful mission. Combined with the equally powerful tool of storytelling, the partnership between the St. Louis Storytelling Festival and the University of Missouri Extension's Community Arts Program makes perfect sense.

I joined the University of Missouri Extension's Community Arts Program in December 2014 when the decision was made to join forces with the St. Louis Storytelling Festival. In an essentially newly created position, I became the University of Missouri Extension Urban Region east community arts specialist and St. Louis Storytelling Festival director. With a background and professional training in folklore, my approach to Community Arts was, and still is, very much about co-collaborative and community-driven programming. In fact, the Festival's history of collaborative programming and community outreach was probably the most appealing aspect of the position. St. Louis has a very rich, complex, and diverse history that continues to evolve in dramatic ways, and I continue to believe that storytelling is such a wonderful way to reflect that history.

From day one of working on the Festival, I was told that there was a "new" relationship being developed with a group in Taiwan, and that we had the opportunity with the 2015 Festival (my first Festival) to incorporate several youth tellers from Taiwan. I was thrilled with this possibility because I could not think of a better opportunity for true exchange learning. I was even more thrilled to learn that a goal was to eventually invite St. Louis youth tellers to Taiwan to participate in the Taiwan Festival. Details were pretty unformed at this early stage, but I liked the direction it was headed.

Over the next two months or so, I learned more and more about how this relationship organically developed between storytellers from St. Louis and groups in Taiwan, and how this was formally developing into an official MOU between the university and MMC Starlight GRC Ltd. in Taiwan. We had an official MOU signing reception during the 2015 Festival, which included the formal exchange of gifts, a formal welcome and greeting between the two organizations (this was the first time I had met the dignitaries from Taiwan face-to-face), and plenty of informal conversation.

For the duration of the Festival, we had several of the youth tellers placed at a few different locations for Festival storytelling sessions. I scheduled them in "teams" that were predetermined by the Taiwanese leadership, and most often, they were accompanied by one of the local tellers (Bobby Norfolk, Sherry Norfolk, Mike Lockett, etc.) who had already worked with some of the youth in Taiwan. In total, each storytelling session lasted for approximately 45 minutes, so it was a good amount of time to sample the short stories of 6–8 Taiwanese youth.

For publicity purposes, whenever I had one of their groups scheduled, I called them "MMC Starlight Goodwill Ambassadors from Taiwan," rather than listing individual names. And at the Grand Finale Showcase concert in 2015, we spontaneously decided to present one very talented youth teller— Joanne Wang on stage with our Festival Featured Tellers. This trend continued for the 2016 Festival as we featured Rosemary Ko on stage at the Finale concert. (*NOTE: I made sure to notify the Featured Tellers of this addition in each case.) Lodging and most logistics for the Taiwanese youth were taken care of by the homestay families at Claymont Elementary. Indeed, there were many activities scheduled at Claymont and elsewhere in the city with Claymont families during the Festival week to allow for a fuller immersive exchange experience for the Taiwan youth, and I had to be mindful of the scheduling.

Those are the basic nuts and bolts of how the MMC Starlight Goodwill Youth Ambassadors were incorporated into the St. Louis Storytelling Festival in 2015 and 2016. Following are a few things I have learned (and continue to learn) as a result of this unique, ongoing exchange.

The St. Louis Storytelling Festival has always emphasized the diversity of cultural heritage revealed through storytelling, and the inclusion of our Taiwanese youth tellers only emphasizes this element. Diverse representations were evident in the beginnings of the Festival, and storytellers continue to be selected to express the rich variety of diverse ethnic, racial, religious, social, and cultural perspectives that have always been present in the St. Louis area. Although the Festival has periodically been able to invite professional featured storytellers from outside the United States, we have never before included international YOUTH participants on this scale. It is unprecedented, to my knowledge. What an amazing asset for the St. Louis community to be able to hear these stories firsthand from not only Taiwanese tellers but also YOUNG Taiwanese tellers! For the Festival, it is a real opportunity to highlight youth as story creators and storytellers in their own right, rather than as just storytelling listeners or participants in a story. Yes, many good professional tellers are highly interactive in their storytelling with youth, and I do not want to suggest otherwise. But as a Festival presenter, we can provide a stage for these culturally diverse youth perspectives, one of the greatest assets of our Festival.

The fact that this is a recurring partnership allows the storytelling exchange to build and deepen over time, one of the hallmarks of building community. Currently, our MOU is structured with a five-year time limit in mind (2015–2020), with the possibility of renewing that MOU partnership again at that time. Already in the second year of this MOU, it is clear that a true international community is developing. Familiar faces return, experiences and stories are shared over time, and we all get an opportunity to see each other grow and to see how the shared experiences are shaping each of us. Particularly for the participating youth, storytelling skill development is at a crucial stage for them. To have the opportunity to be shaped at this critical age by these experiences over time truly becomes a part of their identity. I know anecdotally from the students at Claymont that they consider their Taiwanese counterparts to be "friends," and that they are truly sad when the guests have to leave. It is easy to plan a one-time exchange, but to have a recurring exchange where ideas, feelings, and experiences can organically grow over time is invaluable and very rare. As a Festival presenter, it will be interesting to see how we can present this aspect of the project on stage.

Regular communication is key! Most would agree that on paper, this is a wonderful opportunity, but few can truly appreciate the enormous amount of planning that must happen for something like this to take place. There are myriad details to consider—logistics of transportation, lodging, language issues, food, financial support, cultural differences, scheduling, and so much more. From a Festival planner's perspective, we had the great benefit of the Claymont School so generously offering homestays for the students. This certainly helped alleviate some of the logistical issues, but it also presented some challenges with scheduling, as we wanted the guest tellers from Taiwan to really be able to spend time with host families. Good communication is the key to making something like that work. Internationally, the communication often had to happen over e-mail, but there were lots of phone calls made at strange times of the day and night.

As we continue the planning now for 2017 and beyond, one thing that is becoming clear to me is the need for regularly scheduled contact, such as a monthly phone call or monthly Skype session. For example, in 2015, St. Louis was visited by 29 Taiwanese youth; in 2016, that number jumped to 42! To ensure that things go smoothly from the perspectives of both sides of the exchange, the communication has to be responsive. Spontaneous communication is useful and indeed is necessary, and both sides need to be available and willing to ask questions as well as answer them whenever they arise, or to put others in touch with the appropriate resources. But regularly planned communication provides a more structured framework. It is also important to realize that each side may have varying deadlines, timelines, and so forth, so it is crucial to keep the lines of communication open.

The coplanning involved in this endeavor is a less visible, yet equally crucial component to the value of this type of exchange. The stories that the youth share, and the storytelling experiences for the youth, are the primary reason why this exchange is happening. It is not only a cultural exchange, but also one that will help the Taiwanese in their English language acquisition. This is the primary component. Yet on a broader scale, there is collaborative learning going on at the institutional level as we engage in this coplanning process.

As a Festival planner, for example, I am curious not only about the many cultural aspects of Taiwanese storytelling but also the cultural aspects of Taiwanese festival and event planning itself. What makes up the institutional framework of their planning process? What are their overall goals? Who are they accountable to? What do their various organizations and institutions want to get out of an exchange like this? These are all important questions to consider, because they are all questions we on the American side have needed to ask ourselves throughout this planning process.

For example, as a community arts specialist, I approach the Festival, and the opportunity to present Taiwanese youth, through a particular lens of community engagement. As a University of Missouri Extension employee, I have certain responsibilities to fulfill in terms of accountability as well as resources available (or not available, in some cases) to me that I otherwise would not have (and some that are not). The schools and venues that the St. Louis Storytelling Festival works with all have their own educational and curricular goals in mind when they agree to host the Taiwanese youth for a session. And I am sure the educators, administration, and families of Claymont have their own objectives, goals, and resources at hand. As all the key players come together for this exchange, we need to be aware what is similarly happening on the Taiwanese side and the framework within which they are working.

Additionally, there is the simple fact of cultural protocols that we need to be aware of. A good example of this is how we welcomed our Taiwanese guests to the Festival in 2015. This became a very formally catered affair, with important university dignitaries invited to come to St. Louis from the main campus in Columbia to sign the MOU, for a formal gift exchange, and for formal speeches in both English and Mandarin. We contacted our Office of International Programs to participate as well, and I learned from them culturally appropriate ways to shake hands, to address guests, and so on. There are many examples of situations like this over the past two years, and a good, ethnographic consideration of the various ways we each engage in Festival planning has been a useful way to approach this partnership.

The goal of the partnership between the University of Missouri Extension Community Arts Program, the St. Louis Storytelling Festival, and MMC Starlight GRC Ltd. is to build an international storytelling community. This is a unique opportunity, one that we look forward to developing.

Aaron Wills, Claymont Elementary

Our world is changing rapidly. If our students are to be successful in this dynamic environment, they will need new skills that may not have been as important for previous generations. As technological innovations cause the world to become more interconnected, our students' skills and experiences must allow them to solve problems at the global level. In fact, our school district's mission is *to ensure that all students are curious, capable, caring, and confident learners who understand and respond to the challenges of an ever-changing world*. Additionally, one of our vision statements is that our students will *always be seeking understanding of the views, values, and cultures of others*. But how do you accomplish that in a suburban midwestern community? How can elementary school students begin to learn about and experience the global community?

Our partnership with Starlight has given us a new avenue to provide essential twenty-first-century learning experiences for our students. When the children from Taiwan spend a week at Claymont, we all get a firsthand, authentic opportunity to build global relationships. As our children work and play together, they learn about languages, cultures, and new perspectives. But children from both countries soon realize that while there are many differences between them, there are many more similarities. It is not long before these strangers from opposite sides of the world begin to learn, play, and laugh together.

Our students benefit greatly from this partnership in so many ways, but it does not come without a lot of preparations. After getting district-level approval, many arrangements had to be made. First, we checked in with the staff and parents to see if they had interest in the project and would lend their support. Then, there were the initial communications to all the school families explaining this new project. Next, we had to seek host families who would be willing to invite two children into their homes for the week. Both years, we had almost enough volunteers to place all the children after the initial request. We then tapped a few more families on the shoulder and asked them directly if they would be willing to host. Some had other obligations during that particular week, but others were

Starlight Goodwill Ambassador tells a story at Claymont's special welcome assembly.

Claymont students welcome their Taiwanese guests in many ways.

willing and excited to help after the personal invitation. Soon, we had a great line-up of families who now had a new experience to share. This helped bring many members of our school community together under a new project. Many new friends were made.

One of the challenges of assigning host families was getting the proper boy/girl ratio to work out. We wanted a host family with boys to be hosting boys, and girls to be hosting girls. A few host families had both boys and girls, which was helpful to give us some options as we got to the end of the list. We also made efforts to get the visiting children together with similarly aged children in the homes. It was nice when the young visitors could be staying at homes that also had young children of a similar age.

All host families signed a document releasing the school and district from liability from participating as a host family. Each adult in the household had to also complete a state and Federal Bureau of Investigation (FBI) background check in order to participate. The background check cost for each family with two adults was approximately $100, paid by the family.

Another task to complete was assigning the visiting students to a homeroom classroom at school. Often times, they could go to class with the host children, but we wanted to be sure that all students at Claymont got to have a visitor from Taiwan in their classroom at some point during the week. Though the Starlight group wanted their students to experience a "normal" week at an American school, the week was far from normal because of the excitement of having the guests! Special assemblies, storytelling opportunities, and extra social time were built into the week to provide the students enough time to build relationships and learn from each other's gifts and experiences.

Claymont students welcome their Taiwanese guests in many ways.

The school's PTO played an essential role in this partnership. Our generous parents provided a luncheon for all the visiting adults on the first day of school and also purchased and made gifts for all the visitors. We quickly learned about the importance and significance of gift giving in the Asian culture. This was just one of the many lessons we learned about international relations.

Our staff and students also played a big role in making this partnership successful. We took this opportunity to allow our fifth-grade students to take on some big leadership roles. Our fifth graders planned and hosted our all-school opening assembly on the first day of the visit. They also gave school tours to the guests and greeted them upon their initial arrival. The teachers also helped a lot by supporting the visiting students in their classrooms throughout the week. The feedback we received over and over from the Taiwanese kids was, "The teachers are so nice!"

From the school's standpoint, the week-long visit takes a lot of work, some sacrifice of the normal routines, and some tricky logistical challenges (imagine having 40 new students arrive on the same day, midyear, with limited English skills!). But in the end, the lessons learned and the relationships that were built made it all worth the effort. I think one of our host parents summed it up best in an e-mail he sent after the conclusion of the visit:

> *We appreciate all that you did with this program. Thank you for allowing us to be a part of it. I did not know what to expect personally, but I am so happy that we were able to participate. The bond that our Taiwanese girls had with my two girls was incredible. It is too bad it was only for a week. We feel that there were true bonds*

made, and we hope we see them again, but know that it is quite possible that we never do. But again, thanks for all that you did in helping make this experience incredible for our family and our exchange students.

"Taiwanese Exchange Students Visit Claymont Elementary" (Allison Wills, Parkway West High School, *Pathfinder*, May 19, 2015)

It might seem scary to travel halfway across the world to spend a week with an unknown family at the age of nine. However, 29 Taiwanese students and 14 chaperones took up the challenge! Sponsored by the Encyclopedia Britannica Company, the MMC Starlight Exchange Program for Taiwanese elementary school students arrived in St. Louis on April 27 after a brief visit to Chicago.

The group came with the world's largest pop-up book (as in the Guinness Book of World Records), prepared to participate in UMSL's International Storytelling Festival. Aaron Wills, principal of Claymont Elementary, was a chief organizer for the exchange.

"Sherry Norfolk is a storyteller who went to Taiwan to work with the Starlight Storytelling Club in Taichung, Taiwan. They told her that they would like to come to America, and Sherry had worked with Claymont before, so she asked us if we would be interested in hosting this group," Wills said.

One of the biggest challenges was finding host families willing to take in a few Taiwanese students.

"We made a video telling [families] about the experience, and several families responded that they would like to host and were very excited about it," Wills said. "In the end, we had one slot left, so we called a few families and we found one more host family to make 14."

The Taiwanese students, on the other hand, prepared for the trip by practicing their storytelling and learning about American culture.

"We practiced [our stories] a lot and we learned what we needed to know overseas, like responsibility and being respectful," Tim, one of the younger exchange students, said.

There were lots of preparations that had to be made by the host families.

"I was nervous, but we bought gifts for them," Suzanne Mercer, a host parent, said. "I was mostly worried about making food that they would like. I didn't want to make something that they wouldn't eat because then they'd be starving."

However, the Claymont and Starlight students got along very well upon their meeting.

"My host family is really good to me," Joanne said, a Taiwanese student. "I've met many friends at Claymont."

The host families reported positive things about their visitors as well.

"They're great kids," Mercer said. "They've enjoyed things that I've just never thought of. They live in the city so they don't see stars, so one night they went out on the trampoline with my girls and they laid and looked at the stars, and that was really cool for them. We've learned a lot from them, they're very sweet girls—very kind—and it's been a really nice experience."

The exchange students learned to adjust both mentally and physically.

"You don't have many tall buildings here. In Taiwan, everyone lives in apartments, not houses, and the weather in Chicago was really cold," Maggie Lin, a Taiwanese chaperone, said. "Some kids have homesickness, and they have to cope with it."

The exchange families had a packed agenda that led them around the city, to places like the Magic House, a Cardinals baseball game and the storytelling festival.

"The Claymont kids have been very excited; they have stayed up late every night playing with their new friends and learning all about the Taiwanese culture, especially, receiving gifts," Wills said. "They also learned a little bit about the language and about their schools, how they're the same and how they're different."

For some host families, the exchange program brought them closer.

"It has forced us to spend more time together this week as we are forced to put our other obligations aside, so that's nice. I think it was just good for all of us to realize that we have to put those other things that we would usually want to do aside to meet new people and have people in our home and make them feel welcome and learn about their culture. We've definitely learned a lot about their culture," Mercer said.

The Taiwanese students gleaned similar cultural experiences from their hosts.

"They have improved a lot in their English speaking and their performing techniques," Lin said.

Looking ahead, the relations between Claymont and Starlight are far from over.

"They very much want us to come visit them in Taichung, and they also want to come back every year," Wills said.

For now, the students are left with a unique cultural experience.

"I love it here! I love the food here, like hamburgers or pizza," Tim said. "And hot dogs. In Taiwan the hotdogs are blech."

All for Stories—All for Education: Creating a Place for Intergenerational Knowledge in the Classroom

Lillian Rodrigues Pang

This workshop was developed and implemented in school classrooms and communities to achieve multiple aims:

- Create intergenerational dialogue in the school or community;
- Raise Parent and Community (P&C) participation for non-English-speaking family members;
- Raise literacy outcomes for participating students/classes, specifically genre analysis and development;
- Language and cultural/self-identity development;
- Public speaking and drama skills;
- Musical intelligence development; and
- Memorization development, specifically identifying your own memorization style.

Our Multicultural Group

The What

At its core, this is a program of teaching and sharing bilingual stories in the multicultural classroom. This program begins with a focus on sharing cultural tales from each student's multiple identities (nationalities/languages) and using these tales as a context for literacy and community engagement.

Students learn to tell the stories in a range of ways utilizing the skills available in the room—the focus is on the spoken word, bilingual telling, and tandem telling. Other skills that are incorporated are circus skills, drawing, singing, percussion, beat boxing, dance, mime, puppetry, and so forth.

This program was developed, piloted, and run in New South Wales, Australia, with classes five and six (10–12-year-olds). The initial iteration of pilot and three schools was funded by BlueScope Steel ($5000), a large local corporation, and the Multicultural Communities Council (in-kind, supervisor, and assessment hours). It was written and implemented by storyteller Lillian Rodrigues Pang. Since then this program has been run in high school and community groups, in particular targeting refugee families entering the country/established community.

The Why

School communities with large, diverse, cultural makeup were finding it hard to engage parents in the education of children. Parental involvement in a child's education is positively associated with academic outcome; this has been recognized worldwide in both research and policy initiatives.

Community groups were finding it hard to share stories and create connection between newly arrived with limited English and the wider community.

Intergenerational connections were difficult among communities where the child spoke strong English and the parent did not. In particular, if the child did not have a strong capability or nuance in the "home" language, disconnection in teenage years was high and disruptive to the family and community.

Refugees were stating that they were not meeting people outside of their own culture/language.

Ta da ta da daaahhhhhh! Welcome to the bilingual storytelling program!

The How

Program Structure Outline

Below is the program structure in stages. You can apply each stage to the amount of time you have available. I have run this as a four-week program with 2.5-hour sessions per week, which is not ideal but doable. Ideal for me is a 10-week program.

Preliminary	Notes and "welcomings"	
Stage One	Storytellers and stories	Performance of stories by the storyteller
One week		Story cascade
		Who? What? When? Where? of stories in our lives.
Continuous	Notes and "welcomings"	Story note to families (reminder to seek stories and invitation to share)
Stage Two	Elements of story	Share what stories have been brought in.
		Share with guests who are bringing in stories. Typically community people come first.
Three weeks		Story cascade
		Make paddle-pop stick puppets for some of the main characters of stories that have been shared.
		Tandem telling—discover and play
		Examine the structure of the story. (Literacy)
		Notions of character
Continuous	Notes and "welcomings"	Here are some characters (photo copy the paddle-pop stick puppets) –Remember? –GREAT—tell us
Stage Three	Voice, language, and expression	Our body and sound explanations/ diagrams/exercises
Three weeks		What can be said without words? Sound/movement/body
		Memorization techniques
Continuous	Notes and "welcomings"	Here are some characters— remember—tell us
Stage Four	Outcomes	Performance
Three weeks		Book production
		Digital production

The Program Structure with Detail

Preliminary

Most importantly you MUST prepare creative, fun, visual notes that can constantly go back to the caregivers via the students. Visual notes because we are trying to engage people with limited English or limited access points to the current school education system. This communication needs to be

Stick Puppets

constant and enticing to bring them past the barriers to entry that they face. The participants' enthusiasm will do the rest.

Notes need to go out early to let families know you will be calling on them. Make these notes distinctly different right from the start. Not just another color of paper—try drawing a story fire and putting info in that, or a tree with their child's face on it and stories as the roots, and so on.

Research the cultural makeup of the classroom/community you are entering and stories from those areas. These may be Celtic, Scottish, German, Italian, Mexican, Cuban, Pipil Indian, Palestinian, Croatian, Jewish, and the like.

Meet with all relevant teachers/leaders (English, homeroom, digital, drama, events, librarian). Understand the behavioral point system in place at any school/library/community organization so you can fit seamlessly into that. Try to integrate other units of learning or activity with the storytelling, for example, Scouts can have a fairytale-themed camp with activities, or the library can have a "community book" and have an event in which the creators read or perform the book.

Stage One: Stories and Storytellers

First, set the example by doing. Present a range of oral stories, selecting from folktales, myth, fairytales, and personal tales.

Keep storytelling performances as simple as possible at first (not too many props) as you want to encourage the understanding that anyone can tell stories, under any circumstances.

Limit the personal tales to character stories—for example, the uncle who always fought the law, the grandmother who could not keep a pair of shoes to save her life, the cousin who paints, and so forth.

In my case, I have a cousin in Palestine who was a lead artist on the 10,000 Kites Project where kids from both sides of the wall painted their dreams onto kites and flew them to intersect over the wall. I tell this story. It has a great cascade effect that also allows us to discuss history and people's hopes for the future and how "political" differences can be put aside by people highly affected by them.

Characters—ask for the characters in their families that they know of. Is it themselves, brother, or is there a story that gets repeated? Is this how you know about overseas people? This part often promotes the "overseas" component of families.

Promote a story cascade—what stories have you heard? Who told them to you? How much of it can you remember/share with the class right now? Where/what country or culture is this story from and in what language did you hear it?

Finish this session examining one story that most cultures share such as "Little Red Riding Hood," "The Tortoise and the Hare," or "The Red Hen."

Traditional stories represented by culturally appropriate images

Admission—I love the Red Hen story. Of the three stories above, I have enjoyed the Red Hen the most. It is a comfortable framework with high levels of repetition.

You can include any number of languages in this story—for example, each character that the Red Hen asks for assistance can be from a different culture. The dog could be Spanish speaking, then the cat Serbian, a lizard Thai, and so forth. That way all members of the class get to learn a little bit of all the languages that are present in the story.

I have found that the story is also a safe structure to discuss our similarities and differences. Typically, the Red Hen feeding her children and no one else at the end is the same in all versions of the story. The story varies in "material" in each culture (corn, wheat, rice) and which animals are present. This offers us a way to talk about differences, the basic food of your culture (chickpea flour, wheat flour, corn flour), and the methods of cooking or inviting someone to eat. For example, in Australia we say "bring a plate"; this is often confusing to people who are new to the Australian culture. For Australians, "bring a plate" means to bring a dish of food to share, so new immigrants typically have a story of when they first encountered this saying and how they literally brought their own (empty) plate to a BBQ.

The resulting language discussions from this story prompt are rich and engaging. It is often surprising for students to learn that the majority of English speakers in the world are not born in English-speaking countries, nor do they learn it as their first language; so we can talk about the changing and shifting nature of the oral story as well as the language we use for orality (such as Spanglish, Tinglish, Chinglish, Singlish).

One modern complexity to note: Often, the first range of stories that I get are from Disney or current movies/series/games. It is often hard to distinguish these from "folktale and personal contributions." Initially, I had to research modern shows, popular games, and the like that utilize characters from cultural stories.

Stage Two: Elements of Story

Right at the beginning when you are preparing, establish who you are inviting into the classroom from the community and organize their visit. Typically, this has been the "cultural elders" such as church leaders, singers/choir masters/dance instructors/martial arts instructors/folk musicians, language teachers, and translators within the department of education.

If any family members come to share straight away, make a safe place and establish the ways to tell stories utilizing a range of languages. Consider which children will translate, if you will get a council or academic translator or local figure, and so forth.

Building on the story cascade is important. Keep this flow going. Share the stories that have been gathered by the students. Build and research those stories so that they feel they can share them. Demonstrate how you track a story down using Google/uni resources, online catalogues, or other sources to scaffold their own personal attempts.

Practice tandem telling and interpretation, with a celebration of the skills of those who can interpret. If need be, employ an interpreter to come in and lead the children's interpretations of stories and to work (if intergenerational and culturally and linguistically diverse [CaLD] engagement is the aim).

Try a gesture game: It is best to use a large puppet. Partner up. One person says a line of the story; then the puppet has to do a move or gesture to encapsulate the mood or emotion of that line. It must be a small movement—a gesture.

With puppets, we convey emotion via symbolic movements, for example, hand on heart; head slightly left; mouth wide open; head tilted to the side; mouth pulled in; head pulled back slightly.

You can play this as a line-by-line story game and have one person in the middle translating the emotion to a puppet gesture for each new line. It is a fun game that is creative and thoughtful and really assists the "teller" to clarify movement.

We examine the structure, detailing the difference between the traditional fairytale and the folktale. We will discuss the turning points in the story and mark them. This is like creating a "choose your own adventure" story. Pick the points where choices are made or could be made. Mark those points. These are the points we can use for drama or pregnant pauses when telling. They are also the points that lead us to learn about the main character.

The class examines notions of character, travelling with the character and relating to the character. Further to this, we develop the character of some of the stories shared earlier; that is, what is the fullest picture of the character we can develop/draw? Think about food/clothing/shopping style/reaction on an athletics field and so forth. Do this with folktales as well as personal tales. What do we know about our family overseas or others whom we did not meet from these stories? What does our storyteller want us to know?

At this stage, we really want to engage the family. Sending home notes in the form of paddle-pop stick puppets (or images of them) tend to lead to questions. Sending in characters from the range of nations/languages might pique an interest or a version of a story (a different ending or addition of another character). Be as creative as possible while sharing the kind of knowledge that you are interested in harnessing. Sending in photos of who is coming in might help as well so they can see "likeness" in the classroom/place.

Sock Puppets

Stage Three: Voice, Language, and Expression

All of us make sound, although few of us know how the sound is made. There are basic diagrams available on the Internet that you can use to explain the production of sound and the function of vocal chords.

From here you can talk about warming up the voice and doing some basic exercises, such as "singing" a favorite song as a "raspberry" (put lips together and roll).

Talk about the proper posture for sound production: chin level, weight on heels and soles of feet, neck loose.

Explore making sounds with an exercise with different notes using "doh," "ray," "me," "fa," "so," "la," "ti," and "doh." Use different mouth shapes and vowels: "ooh," "ee," "a," and "aah." Try singing up and down a scale (called an arpeggio). Sing short (staccato) notes as well as long ones.

I play beatboxing games here as well. I find the videos of Mal Webb extremely fun at this point. Mal Webb is a dynamic and inspiring Australian artist who has a YouTube channel. Mal has a video of himself beatboxing, while he has a camera down his throat! Being able to show 10–12–year-olds the vocal cords of someone as they beatbox is fascinating and highly memorable (https://www.youtube.com/watch?v=faAtOul8euQef).

Share stories gathered by students, trying out some of the vocal techniques as you go. Tell the story slouching on a chair, and then tell it with good posture; tell it in a high-pitched voice; tell it as a bear.

Look at sound, body movement, and dramatization, in particular what can be said without words—bringing musical instruments, puppets, and sounds into the delivery of a story.

Consider rhythms and feeling. Practice moving to different beats—slow march, reggae, 4/4, 6/8, heavy metal. Practice telling a line of a story with these different beats.

Suggested Games

Speed sound: One person says a noun, the other vocalizes the sound as quickly as possible, for example, lion, wind, butterfly, whale. Play in a circle and pass it in any direction. You can also include emotions (abstract nouns).

Percussion storm: Start by rubbing the tips of your fingers together, then clicking, then hands rubbing on knees, and then banging on knees. You can search for examples of this as many orchestras or groups do it, and it is fun. It is a great way to demonstrate the power of sounds and interactivity over use of words.

Sound bath: Create a circle with one person in the middle. The person in the center calls the sound that the people in the circle will make as they close in on them, such as flight, angry pigeon, train, turtles, green. Every person in the circle must make the sound that comes to mind that expresses the word of the center person. They make the sound while moving toward that person. The only rule is no aggression.

Exploring Memorization Skills

All stories are told orally from memory, not from a written text. It is good to examine all the memorization techniques available to us and which ones work best for whom.

- Visual spatial intelligence, such as memorizing the main elements of the story in movie sequence and drawing story maps (of either locations or emotions)

- Oral intelligence, such as hearing themselves read the story or some-one else telling the story
- Kinesthetic methods, such as acting out the story and writing the story
- Visual methods, such as telling story with props

This focus on teaching students about their learning and memory processes aids in their self-regulation processes—that is, teaching them about how they learn and the methods that will suit them when approaching education (Root-Bernstein and Root-Bernstein 2001). This helps language learners in the community as well as they discover or reinforce knowledge about the methods they have been using to memorize English.

By participating in these lessons, students will awaken and exercise their musical intelligence. By telling and hearing stories, they will learn to "hear between the lines" (Herman 2002) while reading and remain more engaged in the text. I believe in consistently naming the "intelligence" that is being used by various participants and in celebrating that intelligence to honor the range that exists in any group. Creating a beat and sound scape is a wonderful way to explore musical intelligence.

Puppet Drums

Stage Four: Outcomes

Performance

Step by step, develop the stories into performance pieces:

- Warm up voices, and join people of various intelligences to perform side by side.
- Specify the roles, props, and storytelling styles. These can be presented at school assemblies or in the wider community if the school is interested.
- Explicitly examine or review how each person memorizes a story or their lines in a story.

Permanent Resource

Develop and present to the school a storybook containing all stories gathered and shared during the program. This book can be held in the library/classroom or community center.

From this book, you can establish a youth reading program in which the 10–12-year-olds read from their book to the 5-year-olds.

Digital Program

All of the created/remembered stories can be used as content in a literacy and digital program.

Family Telling

Flow-On Effects: Youth and Identity

This cultural storytelling unit will develop a rich source of materials among the participants. It will call on participants to utilize and enhance their mental skills such as imaging, thinking, analyzing, and modeling. They will actively engage in conversation with other community members, creating an intergenerational dialogue. The participants will have the opportunity to learn more about their cultural heritage while actively forming a dynamic view of their own cultural identity and the elements that may come to play in its formation.

Storytelling in this program offers a place to form connection, to find and accept our similarities and differences, and to value all of them as a unique story (Bolitho and Hutchinson 1998). The strength of looking to cultural stories is that it allows us to claim what relates to us in this modern-day society and reshape it by our current experience. Learning the form of story offers our children a way of shaping and identifying their own experiences.

Bibliography

Bolitho, Annie, and Mary Hutchinson. *Out of the Ordinary: Inventive Ways of Bringing Communities, Their Stories and Audiences to Light.* Curtin, A.C.T.: Canberra Stories Group, 1998.

Herman, Gail. "Lesson Plan: Sound Effects." *YES! Youth, Educators & Storytellers Alliance* "Lesson Plans," 2002. http://yesalliance.org/resources/lesson-plans.

Root-Bernstein, Robert S., and Michele M. Root-Bernstein. *Sparks of Genius: The Thirteen Thinking Tools of the World's Most Creative People.* New York: Mariner, 2001.

2
Voices of Our Elders

A people without the knowledge of their past history, origin and culture is like a tree without roots.

—Marcus Garvey

Editors' Comments

In his article below, "The Elders Circle," Jim May sums up the significance of listening to the stories of our elders: "When an elder dies, it is like a library burning down." Every day, the stories of families, lives, communities, and events are lost to posterity because no one was listening.

This is *not* happening in the communities described in this chapter. Here you will encounter storytellers who not only understand the importance of listening to their elders but also have developed and nurtured multiple opportunities for the stories to be heard by others. In the process, communities have been strengthened, enriched, and transformed.

"A library is not a luxury but one of the necessities of life," said Henry Ward Beecher. These articles will inspire and empower you to preserve the "libraries" in your community!

Elders Tell

Lynn Rubright

> *I want to awaken the passion and creativity of youth, combine it with the wisdom, experience and insight of elders, and transform our world.*
>
> —Ocean Robbins

We seek the wisdom, experience, and insight of elders by seeking out—and listening to—their stories. Powerful storytelling is happening today through NPR programs like *This American Life*, *The Moth*, and TED talks both on radio and YouTube. Dr. Lee Ann Woolery, an assistant professor at the University of Missouri Extension and specialist for state arts programs, is piloting special community projects in rural Missouri towns to preserve stories and music that reflect a community's local culture. The annual St. Louis Storytelling Festival builds bridges between young and old.

This article explores three successful St. Louis projects designed to transform our world through listening to the wisdom of the elders. With imagination and leadership, all of these programs can be replicated at schools, libraries, churches, and community and cultural centers.

The Centenarians

My husband, Robert, former university professor, writer, public speaker, and reporter, approached the ministers of our church with an idea: "Let's have a church storytelling program that celebrates the stories of our two centenarians." He volunteered to organize the event and publicize it to our members and the community. Ministers agreed to offer a church luncheon for $5 per person in our fellowship hall prior to the event.

Robert sent our two vibrant, articulate, and humorous elders a questionnaire to help them prepare to tell about events in their lives. Topics included adages they lived by; embarrassing moments; emigrant tales or stories of moving and relocation; everyday rituals; family heirlooms; fortunes lost and found; holidays; family traditions; milestones like courtships, weddings, and births; funerals; pet and animal stories; changes in transportation; and turning points. He also interviewed the ladies in person at their retirement centers to help them focus on memorable moments they wanted to pass on through their stories.

The program captured the imaginations of members of our congregation. They flocked into fellowship hall, buffet lunches in hand, filling 20 tables of 8 to listen to the poignant stories of a century of living. Robert served as interviewer/provocateur to provide energy and humorous commentary of his own to keep the stories flowing. The audience loved it. They wanted more. The next year he developed another storytelling program to include a "show" in which the preachers told stories of their own lives.

These were low-budget events that enriched the congregation, proving the old adage that when you know someone's story your heart is opened in a new way. Listening to stories can build bridges to understanding, lead to appreciation of our differences, and increase tolerance and even the possibility of forgiveness.

Such storytelling events are low cost, and with planning and imagination, they can be replicated at community centers, libraries, and schools. Publicity through the church bulletins, newsletters, Facebook, Twitter, e-mail, and the local newspapers is crucial to getting a crowd.

Funding sources for a variety of community-storytelling events can be small grants, advance tickets, freewill offerings, or funds from an organization's annual budget for educational programming and entertainment.

Eldertel

Many years ago, Marilyn Probe, St. Louis poet, storyteller, visionary, and "community organizer," created a successful eight-week storytelling program called Eldertel. It brought together underserved older citizens who frequented a north St. Louis community center and sixth graders from a nearby school. "My main objective was to encourage both young and older members of the audience to research, write and *tell* their own stories to each other." Marilyn hoped intergenerational storytelling would break down barriers of shyness and lead to friendships between young and old participating in the program. She envisioned that youngsters listening to tales of hardship and unusual experiences growing up decades ago would help them appreciate the wisdom and values of the elders.

Planning with the teachers from the local school took place several weeks before implementation of the eight-week program at the community center where students and elders met weekly with professional storytellers. Marilyn and the teachers hoped that Eldertel would help their sixth-grade students meet the language arts curriculum objectives by developing skills in listening, speaking, writing, reading, and performing as designated by the National Council of Teachers of English (NCTE).

During the first two weeks of Eldertel, I told several of my own inspirational family stories to demonstrate that people of diverse cultural and socioeconomic backgrounds have similar concerns, hopes, and dreams.

In the third week, Gladys Coggswell, a specialist in African American stories and a Missouri Folk Arts Program scholar, demonstrated how telling a story using music and movement breaks down barriers between generations and helps them bond and appreciate each other. She invited the audience to join her in singing and dancing an old spiritual, "In That Great Day Gettin' Up in the Morning." Gladys asked the elders if they had danced when they were young. (Of course some of our elders were not mobile, but they enjoyed the action from their seats.)

Nonie, a woman in her 50s who had brought her mother to the program, raised her hand and told how as a child she had been paralyzed and was told she would never walk again. Gladys urged Nonie to come up front and tell her story. "Look at me now!" Nonie said, spinning around the room, "I became a model and a dancer. What you children need to know is that you can achieve anything with the help of your parents, your friends, and your teachers. But you have to believe in yourselves."

"How many of you children know how to dance the Charleston?" asked Nonie. The children had never heard of this dance, but the elders nodded. Soon Nonie had almost everyone dancing the Charleston. "Now let's learn the soft shoe." Gladys tapped the tambourine as everybody danced.

When the two-hour session was over, Gladys said, "When you children go home today, interview grandparents and elders you know, asking them to tell you about the Charleston and the soft shoe dances they did when they were young. Write down their stories. Show them you know those dances, too. And next week when I return, I want you to read or tell their stories."

Probe funded Eldertel by cobbling together small grants from the Missouri Arts Council, Missouri Humanities Council, and the St. Louis Regional Arts Commission. With creative leadership, the basic idea for an intergenerational storytelling program can be replicated by forming collaboratives between schools, libraries, and community and cultural centers. If such a project entails funding from a local education or arts agency, planning a year in advance is recommended for meeting grant deadlines.

Eldertel reminded me of a remarkable oral history project that evolved and lasted the entire school year in a fifth-grade class when I was director of Project TELL (Teaching English through Living Language) in the Kirkwood, Missouri, school district.

Kirkwood as It Was (1895–1929): Meramec Highlands—An Oral History Storytelling Project with Students and Elders

One morning Eddy rushed into Leslie Handley's fifth-grade class and dumped shards of broken pottery and bent cutlery onto her desk. "Mrs. Handley, look what I found when I was exploring near the old abandoned railroad tracks behind my house. My mother said these might have been used at the Meramec Highlands Resort that burned down in 1929. Our house is one of the cottages on the grounds of the Highlands where St. Louis families came by train or trolley for their vacations every year."

"What you have here might be artifacts from the site of the hotel," said Handley, who suggested the children go on a dig to find more remnants from the resort. As part of a math project, the children made wooden squares with screens to sift dirt and residue from the things they might dig up. A local TV station got wind of the dig and brought cameras to record the adventure for the five o'clock evening news report. Children labeled and classified their findings and placed them on tables outside of Handley's classroom as the science/social studies component of an evolving oral history project.

The story of Handley's students' dig on the nightly TV news spread the word of the Meramec Highlands oral history storytelling project. To increase interest and encourage community participation, students wrote ads and placed them in local neighborhood newspapers inviting elders with memories of Meramec Highlands to come to the school to tell their stories and be interviewed. Dozens of elders responded and agreed to come to Handley's class to share their memories of going to the Highlands as children.

At Ms. Handley's request, an educator from the Missouri Historical Society Members came to Handley's classroom to train the children in proper and effective techniques for gathering oral histories: how to use the tape recorder; to *always* ask *open-ended questions* that led to more information and could not be answered with a simple *yes* or *no*; and *always* get a person's name and address correctly spelled as well as a signed permission slip giving the school the right to transcribe the stories and print them in the booklet the children were "publishing."

Elders who could not come to the school welcomed children, with their parents, to come to their homes to listen to their stories and interview them. Parents also helped the children transcribe the stories from tape recorders. The project necessitated doing additional research on the Meramec Highlands at the local library and the Kirkwood Historical Society. As the body of information increased, the children worked tirelessly revising and editing the stories they were gathering.

As the project progressed, the elders periodically came to the classroom to review the stories collected and help deepen the understanding of how important Meramec Highlands had been to them as children. When they brought diaries and photographs to share, the Meramec Highlands project evolved into a unit on photojournalism. The book written by the children in Ms. Handley's class, based on the oral histories and research they had done, was called *Kirkwood as It Was (1895–1925): Meramec Highlands*—and it now included photographs. The Parent Teacher Organization (PTO) and the school principal came up with funds to publish copies for each child and the elders who contributed history, stories, and pictures.

In May, the year-long oral history storytelling project that had begun with a few shards Eddy had found and put on Ms. Handley's desk was now complete. Children sent invitations inviting everyone involved in the project to a "book signing" tea in Ms. Handley's classroom. The elders and everyone else who helped received signed copies of the book the children had researched and written. As a special treat, several of the elders who by now the children knew to be "great storytellers" were invited to share some of their favorite memories.

Ms. Handley had successfully kept the project going all year long by interlacing language arts, social studies, mathematics, and science curriculum. She demonstrated how one topic, initiated by one child, could lead to motivational experiential learning.

Working closely with Ms. Handley, when I was director of Project TELL in her school district, taught me that the spark to initiate an innovative interdisciplinary storytelling project that involved the community could be a parent, an administrator, a teacher, a senior citizen, or a child, like Eddy. The key to the success of the Meramec Highlands project was the leadership of Ms. Handley. Her sense of adventure, enthusiasm, and humor and her courage to risk innovation are rare today in schools, where test-based standards too often limit a teacher's creativity and are time consuming. The Meramec Highlands project demonstrates that students and elders in a community can grow and learn together.

Ultimately, Ms. Handley was awarded the National Social Studies Teacher of the Year Award, in part due to her imaginative development of the Meramec Highlands project in a Kirkwood, Missouri, elementary fifth-grade classroom.

Bibliography

Rubright, Lynn. *Beyond the Beanstalk: Interdisciplinary Learning through Storytelling*. Out of print. Portsmouth, NH: Heinemann, 1996. Chapters 10, 11, 12, pp. 75–96.

The Elders Circle

Jim May

When an elder dies, it is like a library burning down. For all of human history, with the exception of past few decades, it was the elders of the family, the tribe, and the village who were depended upon to preserve and transmit the history, beliefs, customs, and moral values of the people. This was all done through the telling of stories. In fact, every major world religion has transmitted their most important concepts through the medium of stories and parables. The indispensable role of the elder was to remember, reconstruct, advise, teach, and initiate the youth so that there could be a continuous thread of culture through time and history, so that each generation could come to know what was important in life and what needed to be done for the survival of the culture. That our ancestors were successful at this task of mentoring and preserving is substantiated not only by the existence of countless folktales, myths, and ballads, traditional music and dance whose origins precede the printing press, but also by the fact that the world's cultures, and knowledge itself, have continued to survive and prosper through the ages, building upon the oral transmission of knowledge from the past.

The Beginnings of the Elders Emphasis

The final years have a very important purpose: the fulfillment and confirmation of one's character. When we open our imaginations to the idea of the ancestor (elder), aging can free us from convention and transform us into a force of nature, releasing our deepest beliefs for the benefit of society. (Hillman 2000)

Illinois Storytelling Inc. (ISI), formerly known as the Illinois Storytelling Festival, is a nonprofit educational organization whose mission is to increase public awareness and appreciation for oral storytelling and to enhance cross-cultural and cross-generational communication through the preservation and perpetuation of the art of storytelling. ISI is the founder and producer of the Illinois Storytelling Festival, an annual event held for the past 17 years in Spring Grove, Illinois. The festival has been funded each year by the Illinois Arts Council and by numerous corporate, educational, and nonprofit groups over the years. ISI received a 1999 commendation for intergenerational programing at the Illinois Department on Aging's Governor's Conference, and in a *Parenting* magazine review, the Illinois Storytelling Festival was described as "one of America's best family events."

For 15 years, the Illinois Storytelling Festival has hosted an elders' tent in which local community elders and sometimes prominent national elders (including members of the original Tuskegee Airmen and environmentalist/NOVA documentary subject, Richard Walker, who kayaked 1,500 miles) recounted stories from their life experiences. The elders segment has become one of the most popular presentations of the weekend.

ISI staff noted certain recurring themes at the elders' tent:

1. The elders telling stories experienced an enhanced appreciation for their own life experience. They reevaluated their life experiences in a new, positive light.

2. A magnetism was created between the elders and youth in the audience.

3. This was an alternative to the usual classroom learning about history.

4. The elders' very presence plus their stories presented a life continuum lesson to all who listened, including the elders themselves.

5. A kind of "cultural healing" took place, which whole families, young and old, enthusiastically embraced, as the elders presented their stories with humor, reflection, and a sense of joyful rediscovering.

First Training Workshops

Given this major epiphany at its festival, ISI decided to encourage elders in McHenry County to share their life experience stories on a regular basis throughout the year. With the goal of helping McHenry County elders develop improved communication and socialization skills and self-esteem and to provide schools, community service groups, and the public with the wonderful experience we had witnessed at the Illinois Storytelling Festival, four separate training workshops, funded by the Illinois Department on Aging, were scheduled from December 1999 to April 2000 and ISI's Storytelling Initiative was born.

At these training workshops, professional storytellers, Jim May and Michael Cotter (a 69-year-old third-generation farmer, whose reminiscence stories have been featured at the Smithsonian and on a video/documentary for cancer and aids patients) told stories of their life experiences. Then the elders were encouraged to share anecdotes and life stories as the workshop unfolded. The training workshops were held at four different sites around McHenry County. Attendance ranged from 30–50 each meeting, with 130 attending over the four-meeting span.

When the four training sessions were completed, the group requested a monthly meeting date with the elders' own stories taking up the agenda.

First Elders Circle

The results of the first regular monthly meeting were overwhelmingly positive, with 30 people attending the session. The average age of the gathering was the early 70s. Guided by ISI staff (gerontology consultant and counselor, Lynda Markut, project coordinator and retired teacher, Judy Challed, and professional storyteller, Jim May), the elders were delighted to share their stories and only disappointed that there was not more time than the three hours scheduled. The meetings have continued every month for almost one year now with 30–40 people attending even in the midst of one of our most severe winters on record. The group named themselves the Memory Makers and now meets the third Wednesday of every month at the Nippersink Library in Richmond, Illinois. This group has become the pilot Elders Circle, which will be the model for replicated Satellite Elders Circles.

Outreach to Schools

Having maintained a relationship over the years with local schools in the Spring Grove, Richmond, Woodstock, and Harvard communities through sponsorship of storytelling programs, most of them at little or no cost to the school, ISI began inviting elders to visit classrooms and storytelling clubs, always in the presence of an ISI staff person who provided guidance and support. The results have been very successful.

Students from schools that the elders visited accompanied elders to the state fair in Springfield and told stories together at the senior's pavilion. Students and seniors were then featured at our annual Illinois Storytelling Festival, and students told stories to elders at the Woodstock Opera House as a fund-raiser for Family Alliance, the primary nonprofit agency serving McHenry County elders.

A Story

One particular story told at our first monthly meeting is worth mentioning here.

Carl and Helen sat to my right in a rough circle made by library tables and chairs. They had been regular attendees at our festival and at these workshops that Michael and I were conducting. I turned to Carl and asked him:

"Carl, do you have a story to tell?"

Carl, a slight man, wiry, in his seventies, didn't speak at first. The room grew quiet.

Then he said, "I was at Omaha Beach on D-Day.

"The silence in the room deepened.

"I was in the second group. The first group went in at 7 o'clock and we were supposed to go in at 8 o'clock, but we went in at 7:30 because that first group didn't do so good.

Some guys couldn't swim. When the landing craft stopped in deep water they sunk with their heavy packs and drowned.

Those of us who got to the beach just keep on moving. I don't know how I made it. You'd look beside you and your buddy would be there and then you'd look again and he would be gone. Some guys would just be torn apart. But you just had to keep goin'."

The rest of the circle listened in reverential silence.

"I made it through that day in Normandy and then all the way through the Battle of the Bulge and Africa."

I thanked Carl, and looked at his wife, Helen.

"Helen, do you have a story?"

"Oh no," she said, "I just come to listen with Carl."

Helen was always with Carl. They'd walk into our meetings, sometimes, hand in hand—a loving couple who had been married for a long time.

"Come on, Helen, you must have a story."

"No," she laughed and patted Carl on the head.

"I'm just so happy to come with Carl to storytelling; and so grateful that he came back from the war."

I asked her one more time, maybe because I had been a classroom teacher and had a hunch.

"Oh come on, Helen, you must have a story."

The smile left Helen's face. She looked around the group, down at her hands and then back at us as she began to speak.

"We had a baby with Down's Syndrome . . . Patty. At first, I didn't understand. They didn't bring me my baby. I kept asking for my baby. Finally, a doctor came in. He was very mean.

He said, 'It is a mongoloid; we will institutionalize her for you.' His words were pointed like arrows. It was as if he was blaming me for having given birth to my child. Carl and I didn't know what to do.

Finally, I remember the day that I told the nun at the hospital that we were taking our Patty home. And I remember the nun smiled and said, 'Good.

'We just didn't know what to do. I picked up a book about Down's Syndrome and would cry every time I read it. Finally, Carl took the book away from me.

He said, 'We're not going to read the book anymore. We are just going to take a little at a time.'

Carl had been to the war and he knew that you just have to take things a step at a time."Then Helen became very quiet. She looked around the room at each of us.

"I want you all to know how much love that child, our Patty, brought into our marriage."

And we all knew. We had seen the proof every time the two of them walked into the room.

Copyright Jim May, 2016. Excerpted from Trail Guide for a Broken Heart. Marion, MI: Parkhurst Brothers, 2016. Used by permission of the publisher.

Referring to our monthly meetings, Helen said, "We look forward to meeting with all our friends and listening to all the stories. It is really a time we look forward to every month."

Place of Honor in the Community

In terms of the mission and goals of ISI and the Elders Initiative, Carl and Helen's story is storytelling at its best: community based, told with the authority that comes with experience, and containing the oral wisdom and imagery to guide others. Because these stories become an invaluable resource to their community, the *visibility of their storytelling returns the elders to their historical place of honor in the community*.

Old age is not an illness but an ascent.
I think of age as a great universalizing force.
It's the only thing we all have in common.
Life is a continuum.

—May Sarton

Bibliography

Hillman, James. *The Force of Character: And the Lasting Life*. New York: Ballantine Books, 2000.

Weaving Community

Cherri Coleman

Water Spider Brings Fire to the Animals
Retold by Cherri Coleman

In the beginning, we had no fire. The many kinds of animal people were cold and it was dark. At last the Thunders, who lived beyond the sky, sent fire down on the back of Lightning, and left it at the bottom of a hollow sycamore tree.

The animal people saw the glow and the smoke but the tree was on an island, and they could not reach it because of the water. So the different kinds of animal people decided they must learn to work together to bring light and warmth to the world.

The beautiful, white Raven was eager to go. "I am strong and powerful. I will do this for the people." Raven flew high, but the smoke was thick and he flew back black and scorched.

He had no fire.

The owls, Screech, Hoot and Horned, went together, but the flames burned so high, they came back with eyes burned red and ringed with white ash.

Still, they had no fire.

Clever Little Snake swam across the water and went inside a hole at the bottom of the tree to reach the fire. Big Snake, the climber, approached from outside but the heat was too much for either of them and they returned charred and always twisting.

And still, they had no fire.

At last the little Water Spider said, "I will go."

The animal people laughed. "The great and powerful, the wise and the crafty have all gone before you. They have faced great danger and terrible trials. Do you believe that one as tiny as you can carry back something as great as fire?"

"We all have the power to carry fire," she said. "We just need the right tools."

So Water Spider spun thread from her body and wove it into a little basket that she fastened on her back. She dove deep in the cool water, and crossed through the grass to the island. She did not try to gather the flames, but instead put just one tiny coal into her basket, and then skittered back across the surface of the water.

And now the animal people had fire.

To this day we gather around that fire to share warmth and light. And while the Raven is still black and the owls are wide eyed, the Water Spider still teaches us that we all have the power to carry fire and bring comfort to the people.

We just need a small spark, and a basket to carry it in.

An inter-generational group explores Cherokee basketry.

Story and Folk Art as Community Building Tools

In the mid-1980s, two social psychologists, McMillan and Chavis, formed a theory that has become the most widely accepted understanding of how communities work. They found that when people share experiences together, they form a long-lasting emotional connection and look forward to more. What is needed, they said, is to manufacture the opportunity for unique, memorable experiences that underline what we all share as humans. They called it the "Sense of Community."

Story is a natural community builder. In fact, the strong emotional bond of a common story is the factor believed to be the "definitive element for true community."

Like story, heritage arts confirm a deep human relationship. When we weave a basket, we connect with all of those who have gone before us because every culture, all through time, and have woven, speaking the common language of over-under, over-under. The world has yet to invent the machine that can weave a basket. Like story, it remains a uniquely human experience.

It can be difficult, when bringing two diverse groups together, to get them to share their personal narrative. But I find if I can get people to sit still long enough, with a basket in front of them, quieting their minds with the rhythm of over-under, over-under...their brains shift into a quieter place and narrative naturally unfolds. As they weave, they pull their communities tighter, sharing their traditions, values, culture, and beliefs with the stories that unfold.

The Story of "Weaving Community"

"Weaving Community" began as a way to address the loss of intergenerational relationships.

A young girl weaves a garden basket recalling the colors of freshly plowed field.

During a long winter, John Nyberg, the director of Historic Rock Castle in Hendersonville, Tennessee, and I gathered a group of women, aged 7–75, at the visitor's center of that beautiful federal-era home. Our goal was to explore women's place in local history, express it in story and folk art, and create a sense of community between three generations.

We began by reaching back to their great-great-grandmothers' letters and diaries, to consider the skills women needed to face the challenges of their daily life and how much we now take for granted. Through the frontier skill of making baskets, we created empathy with a small part of that life and explored the way time has changed our communication, food ways, and gender roles. We collected stories of women past and present and then reinterpreted the baskets to reflect our own stories of modern life.

As we wove, the group learned to listen, interview, discuss, and narrate. They looked at how their own unique lifestyle and their generational experience made them relate differently, while the shared experiences of food, family, work, and play connected them to each other and to all the generations of women before them.

As we wove and told, we came to recognize that stories, like baskets, are an expression of daily life. And that, like the baskets, narrative changes in form and function according to need, cultural background, and the world around us. As our life changes, so does our relation to story and art.

We harvested their stories and made them tangible. A basket that historically held letters from home became a charging station for a cell phone. A wood splint egg basket was rewoven with plastic grocery bags to illustrate an oral narrative of a family's move from farm to city. The baskets became physical memory aids. The women and girls could look at the basket and recount the story.

Our best moments happened spontaneously. We encouraged the group to go out to lunch together, or to bring food with a story behind it for a potluck meal with a guest speaker: anything to coax out a memory or a tale. When the guest speaker for my "Hen Basket" session cancelled, I made a desperate call to my husband, who put the rather unconventional "speaker" in the car and drove in record time to our classroom. One of the senior students tells it best:

> *I was tired. I didn't feel good, the basket was hard and I'm not chatty. But when she took that (live) chicken out of the box and asked it to say a few words I was done in. And it did. It talked back. Just sat there in the crook of her arm and clucked back to everybody's questions. I figured if the chicken could do it, so could I.*

As trust and humor built, the women began to open up and influence each other. The teens and preteens took relationship advice from the older women. The high school girls supervised a new haircut for an elder. Peer review of the stories and basket work became focused on bringing out the best each had to offer, rather than "doing it right." Their stories and baskets began to contain small references to other members of the group.

Yet, the tighter we grew, the more we began to expand. The participants began to invite their brothers, husbands, and friends to drop in to listen and see what they were doing. By the next year, the program had expanded to a multicultural social justice focus and included several young men.

As the project drew to a close, we celebrated. The director of Rock Castle, John Nyberg, honored the ladies with an exhibition of basket and story. An artist reception was held for the whole neighborhood, complete with music and sparkling cider. Each participant wore a name tag reading "Artist" as well as a feather boa, chosen to honor the chicken. We had a shared sense of identity, a shared sense of accomplishment, and an inside joke. What more could we ask for?

And all the while, Historic Rock Castle had provided a safe, warm environment for spontaneous conversations between the generations—a place they continued to cherish as their own, while they harvested their personal folklore and reclaimed the long history of what it meant to be a community of women.

What We Learned: Designing Story Programs That Build Authentic Community

Determine Who You Will Serve

The need to be included is universal—regardless of income, age or physical challenges. To present a program like "Weaving Community," first identify who you are best equipped to serve and why. Then take a good look at yourself and your organization. Keep in mind ways that you can be more welcoming of underrepresented voices in your community and be honest about how you may have excluded them in the past. Identify the issue, and brainstorm ways you might create an experience that will bring people together.

Include Community Voice as You Plan

My favorite inclusion mantra is "Nothing about us without us." Talk to your potential participants as you design your program. Their voice is essential to good participation, building bridges and eventually, creating positive change. A good project planner will hear their voices and include them in the planning, development, and launching of the program. Think of the community as a partner rather than a recipient, and accept that that they may guide the project in unexpected and exciting ways.

Unite Your Leaders

Finding common ground with your community, the presenting organization and the teaching artist will create an atmosphere of trust and allow people to work together simply and comfortably. A strong program will reflect the best of the beliefs, values, and lifestyles of all the providers and be more attractive to your funders.

Include Funders as Part of Your Community

Take a look at the strategic plan of your potential funding sources. "Weaving Community" was funded almost entirely by a grant from the Tennessee Arts Commission, even though it was a small, unusual project. Because we made an effort to "promote and support the art of storytelling and basket making and its long and unique history within our state" and reached out to the "traditionally underserved and underrepresented"— namely, youth and elders—we aligned with the Arts Commission's strategic goals. Adding visual arts standards with a folk emphasis strengthened it even further. They were happy to fund us, and we were grateful for the support. The state commission became a partner, rather than just a funding source, and was invited to celebrate with us as we achieved our goal.

Invite, Reach Out, and Collaborate

Reach out to the entire community—family, schools, elders, youth, businesses—and invite participation. Partner with similar groups, and share mailing lists to assure the whole neighborhood is invited to the table. What "in-kind" contributions can be easily tapped, and what partners in the community might be willing to assist?

In our case, the local Senior Center was happy to help with transportation, and a local elementary school helped us identify students who would be excited about taking part. Former students of mine helped keep costs down by volunteering to prepare the basket kits, and a local grocery store provided donations of food, peach tea, and hot chocolate. If your program has a fee, consider offering a few scholarship spots in your program, and invite partners who would be glad to fund them to join in the project.

Be Sensitive to Time-Related Challenges

When is your project taking place? Identify several possible dates in case of conflicts, and consider the time of day. Investigate the unique needs of your participants and partners. In our case, after-school activities had to be considered; so did driving at night for our seniors. The sponsoring partner, a historic home, had a need to increase traffic during the winter months. By holding the workshop during the winter, we were able to help our sponsor and provide a cozy activity for what were often lonely, isolated weekends.

Go Multidiscipline

Adding basketry to story gave the project a visual arts component, which strengthened the grant proposal and added value for the participants. Our location at Historic Rock Castle also added an element of history and folklore, along with the beautiful setting. When you combine the needs of a neighborhood with shared arts experiences, the art can become a tool to help you draw out dialogue, narrative, and relationships.

Keep It Simple

Be realistic about the scale of your program. Keep it small and meaningful. It is better to plan for long-term sustainability than sporadic events. Plan so that when the program is over, youth, elders, and other vulnerable community members will still have a sense of place and belonging.

The first "Weaving Community" project was only five-day-long workshops, with a limit of 15 participants. By the second year, the program had a waiting list, and members would often gift their seats to others if they had to be absent. It was not unusual for people to be standing outside the room to watch or for former participants to stop by and visit. Keeping the program small not only made it simple for the presenters to repeat but also kept it special to the participants and the community.

Locate a Safe, Welcoming Location for the Project

Do your best to create a safe haven—a sense of place, identity, and belonging. The location you choose should feel safe, warm, and inviting. The staff should be gracious, warm, and welcoming, with a good sense of humor and a genuine enjoyment of the participants. The best environment will be welcoming to youth, respectful of elders, accessible to people with handicaps, and inclusive to the community as it changes and grows.

If you are limited to a stark room that is less than cozy, provide a banner or item that visually claims the space as special for the group. And then add some music, coffee, and other comforts to soothe the senses. In the second "Weaving Community" session, we worked with sweetgrass. The aroma had such a wonderful effect on my students that I now bring it with me to all my workshops. As one of the younger girls put it, "Ah, it smells like time to tell a story."

Create Opportunities for Success

Assure that the program is empowering. Set out to foster new skills, communication, and positive social interaction by choosing activities that set participants up for success. They should be achievable, yet respect the unlimited potential that resides in all of your students. Nurture their skills, confidence, and character; create multiple opportunities for story inspiration (i.e., the shared food and our "guest chicken"); and then allow the narrative, baskets, and relationships to take shape.

Include Celebration, Praise, and Reflection

Bringing the community together to celebrate is one of the best parts of the project. Make opportunities to share progress as well as the end result.

Take time also to reflect on the importance of mentors and new relationships and to honor the efforts of the presenting organization. A good celebration recognizes all participants and partners and praises them as valued and respected assets to the community.

Let Your Community Direct Your Growth

Continually seek input from your community, allowing the program to change and evolve naturally in the community it serves. Share the power, success, and responsibility for the program with the participants, their families, the teaching artist, and the larger community. All partners should feel free to offer respectful feedback without fear of being negativity received.

In Closing

Story Programs Foster Lasting Relationships for Individuals, Organizations, and the Community

Story and heritage arts programs provide experiences that encourage dialogue, build trust, and foster empathy. The shared experience of exploring these ancient arts creates an atmosphere that encourages positive interaction between different ages and different interests while emphasizing what it is to be human. When all goes well, we can provide a safe place for the community to nurture itself and to craft their own happily ever after.

Bibliography

May, Jim. *Trail Guide for a Broken Heart.* Marion, MI: Parkhurst Brothers, 2016.

McMillan, David W., and David M. Chavis. "Sense of Community: A Definition and Theory." *Journal of Community Psychology* 14 (January 1986), pp. 6–23.

3

Voices of Cultural Pride

One of the most potent forces for bringing a community together is sharing stories with each other. Storytelling allows a community to shift from thinking of its problems as individualistic to realizing how they fit together into collective patterns.

—Nelda K. Pearson

Editors' Comments

Exploring the history, the music, the stories, and the handiwork—the *culture* of our group—can facilitate social cohesion, foster a sense of belonging, develop a sense of identity, and preserve collective memory.

The projects described in these essays demonstrate the power of storytelling to strengthen cultural pride and community by providing a vehicle for spreading awareness, deepening understanding, and celebration of a shared culture. Through storytelling, people become active participants in their group, learning to express significant aspects of their traditions and spread their cultural knowledge.

Having pride in a particular ethnicity means spreading cultural awareness to the community through leadership, determination, dedication, and passion.

—http://wiki.answers.com/Q/What_is_Cultural_pride

In other words, it means *telling the story*!

Storytellers as Community Cultural Ambassadors

Karen Abdul-Malik a.k.a. Queen Nur

The Family, Fun & Folklife Workshop Series is an applied storytelling model that merges storytelling with other traditional folk culture as a catalyst for cultural sustainability and social change. It is a program in which storytelling and other folk arts intertwine with social entrepreneurship for creative placemaking. The storyteller leads the design by engaging the community, facilitating partnerships, and managing the telling and listening processes. In short, the storyteller becomes a community cultural ambassador.

Definitions

The birthing of the disciplines in this essay parallel the New Age, thereby the definitions are new and evolving. However, there are generally accepted terms that form foundations in applied storytelling, social entrepreneurship, cultural sustainability, and creative placemaking.

Applied Storytelling

Storytelling applications are answers to communal human needs. The community recognizes the answer storytelling carries for those needs and seeks the people who can carry the task of answering the demand. "Applied storytelling is taking storytelling as is and applying it onto a human need" (Shiponi 2011).

Cultural Sustainability

The word "sustainable" has been doing some pretty heavy lifting lately. Industry articles, blogs, and websites address responsible, sustainable living, chiefly in response to the threat of growing world populations and diminishing natural resources. Wikipedia identifies cultural sustainability as "a new interdisciplinary approach aimed to raise the significance of culture and its factors in local, regional and global sustainable development." The National Parks Service's internal cultural resource management guidelines define culture as "a system of behaviors, values, ideologies and social arrangements." Within this basic definition of culture lies a direct correlation to identity. Therefore, cultural sustainability as defined in this article is a definitive set of ideas and actions designed to maintain the viability of values, behaviors, ideologies, and social arrangements.

Social Entrepreneurship

"Social entrepreneurship is the leadership by people working together to solve large problems, social or environmental, without waiting for government or the private sector to lead the way or find them" (Light 2008).

While many descriptors contend that social entrepreneurs are driven to *cause* change, Peter Drucker, a predominant leader in the field, defines it as the ability to *search* for change and exploit opportunities for change (Dees, Emerson, and Economy 2001). For application to the model in this study, social entrepreneurship is defined as a storytelling project with a social mission and visionary leadership that engages opportunities for change.

Creative Placemaking

The National Endowment for the Arts uses the description of Ann Markusen and Anne Gadwa Nicodemus from *Creative Placemaking*. "In creative placemaking, public, private, not-for-profit, and community sectors partner to strategically shape the physical and social character of a neighborhood, town, tribe, city, or region around arts and cultural activities." Tom Borrup adds that creative community building involves never-ending work of building and rebuilding the social, civic, physical, economic, and spiritual fabrics of communities by weaving multiple endeavors, professions, and the best practices of varying fields. Creative placemaking in the Family, Fun & Folklife Workshop Series identifies the storyteller as the cultural ambassador that ignites community building around storytelling and other folk arts.

Need

The Family, Fun & Folklife Workshop Series pursues the question: What are the possibilities of rebuilding or sustaining thriving communities if we think about systems that enfold storytelling and other folklife traditions into their processes?

With the economic, social, and cultural deficiencies in our communities, there is a need for storytellers and other teaching folk artists to become or reclaim their roles as community cultural ambassadors; to use their art forms to stimulate civic engagement; and to help community members find solutions to community problems through their rich traditions. A study convened by *Champions of Change* evidenced that "the experiences we offer to many young people outside of school are often limited in their purpose and resulting impact. They provide recreation, but no sense of creation. They provide recess, but no sense of success. Conferring on community members a vital sense of identity, belonging, and purpose, folklife defends against social disorders ... Traditions do not simply pass along unchanged. In the hands of those who practice them they may be vigorously remodeled, woven into the present, and laden with new meanings" (Arts Education Partnership 1999).

When culture and tradition are not honored and maintained, social and moral identity is compromised and value systems are weakened. In these conditions, mankind unravels its life support, and, cultural, social, and economic systems become unsustainable. To survive, we must engage in activities that sustain our culture and disengage in customs that destroy our humanity and environment.

Storytelling is the heart of cultural sustainability. The telling of our stories evokes revelation within and intimacy without. It is how we connect and an instrument for passing on legacies that come from the hand and heart. It can tell us how we got to the edge, and it is what can bring us back like the natural transition of night into day. Storytelling is used to build, change, transform, and sustain. Stories project images of collective experiences and contain the quintessence of creation—the rhythm of life.

Programs that use storytelling as a primary source of seeking resolution inherently create opportunities for relationship building. Relationships are the key element in creating sustainable environments. "The performance of stories coalesces relationships across time and space and creates shared experiences" (Langellier and Peterson 2004). Most of human history is transmitted through the art of storytelling. The stories that we tell and the stories that we listen to are ingrained in who we are and how we live. In return, our identity and means of survival are ingrained in the stories that we listen to and the stories that we tell. Storytelling enables a social process that in turn enables cultural sustainability.

The gift of storytelling has the incomparable ability to move us into collective action. Ancestor Brother Blue, hailed as the father of American storytelling said, "If I had children, this is what I would tell them to do. Be on the case—Trying to do the work. Because you see darling, each of us be the one we are looking for. Go about touching human hearts. Get pass the axiom of birth. Get pass your particular gender, your particular vision, ethnicity. Be a truth walker. Act like you are here to change the world" (Black Storytellers Speak, 2000).

Family, Fun & Folklife Workshop Series

Scope

The Family, Fun & Folklife Workshop Series is designed as a replicable model for storytellers to "be on the case" one community at a time. It innovatively seeks to merge storytelling and other traditional folk culture as a catalyst for social change by building creative spaces for folk artists to serve as community cultural ambassadors. It is an eight-week series that begins in October and culminates in an exhibition and performance at the Annual Willingboro Kwanzaa Festival during the last week of December. The project is produced by In FACT Inc.: Innovative Solutions through Folk Art, Culture and Tradition, a 501(c)3 that I founded in 2011 while matriculating a masters in cultural sustainability at Goucher College.

The project was engendered in 2012 and is in its fourth year of implementation in Willingboro, New Jersey, a predominately African American suburban community. The Family, Fun & Folklife concept is unique to Willingboro. Interviews with township administrators affirmed that youth and senior programs do not converge. Family, Fun & Folklife provides an environment that marries the openness of the beginner with the wisdom of experience while promoting mutual appreciation and understanding. By infusing the oral tradition in intergenerational settings that teach folklife traditions, elders are able to provide the opportunity to use life experiences to communicate history, knowledge, and wisdom to youth in ways that youth might not otherwise countenance. The cultural competency of Family, Fun & Folklife is an asset to the township's initiatives to encourage community involvement, increase youth programming, and generate new family programming.

On a larger scale, the program presents a replicable model in any community. Family, Fun & Folklife is not designed to replace or compete with other programs. The collaborative nature of the project seeks to elevate community folklife and combine economic, political, social, and cultural resources to address concerns that are prevalent within the community, by identifying, building awareness of, and utilizing its collective assets.

Goals

- Strengthen families and communities
- Enrich and empower community life
- Preserve and sustain storytelling and folk arts traditions
- Use storytelling and folk arts to ignite change

Objectives

- Create a community arts-in-practice model
- Build community partnerships and collaborative arts practices
- Build awareness of community assets and needs
- Forge intergenerational relationships
- Combine resources and generate programs seeking innovative solutions for existing community organizations
- Produce an exhibition and concert featuring new social art work
- Create a documentary and workbook for replication of model

Design

There are four phases to the project.

Phase I—Discovery

It is imperative for the success of any community-building project that the stakeholders are invited to the creative process. Although as the artist/storyteller/community cultural ambassador you may live in the community being served, you cannot build the project solely based on your assumptions and ideas about that community. To truly know a community's story, there must be a collective gathering of individual stories to recognize and acknowledge the treasurers of its traditions. Your planning process must begin with the fieldwork.

With the help of folklorist Thomas Carroll and the partnership of the Perkins Center of the Arts, Moorestown, New Jersey, we sought out the "gatekeepers" of the community and asked for further recommendations. We talked to local government officials and administrators; held three focus groups; and, interviewed artists. It was through these conversations that we learned of valuable assets in our community as well as social issues that community members felt needed to be addressed.

Jill Cyrus, director of the Willingboro Recreation Department, is passionate about families getting back to the basics. "The economic situation means that we have to do more with less. Increased gas prices mean families have to do more at home." Kendall Brunson, the assistant director, revealed, "Although we provide performance art and sports for our youth we need cultural programming. Additionally, the township youth programs and senior programs don't have collaborative projects." The mayor at the time, Jacqueline Jennings, concurred, "Our community needs more exposure to culture allowing us to celebrate our differences and similarities. We need programs in which culture can be learned."

The Willingboro Recreation Center provides free space and advertises the project, and administrators became part of the planning committee.

Phase II—Planning and Implementation

With the collected stories, data, identified community folk artists, and potential partners, the next action steps are put in place. In this phase, the storyteller as community cultural ambassador leads the planning team that now includes members from the community and meets with master artists, the media, and partners.

The only predetermined folk arts discipline is storytelling. Storytelling is integrated into each folk arts workshop and is a stand-alone workshop for children.

In each specialized workshop there are three focus areas:

1. Exposure to and learning the skill of the art form
2. Create new works that speak to social justice issues
3. Share stories and traditions simultaneously

Through discovery, the folk arts identified were: praise dancing, quilting, jazz, the blues, basketweaving, hair braiding, dollmaking, soul line dancing, African dance (Liberia), hip hop, drumming, folk medicine, soap making, African and African American food culture, and gardening.

In the initial year, 2012, the committee selected dollmaking (Alma Day), quilting (Winnie Thomas), hip hop and the blues (Sarai Abdul-Malik), and storytelling (Karen Abdul-Malik).

All sessions are 90 minutes with the exception of quilting, which is designed in three-hour sessions. The workshops are offered free of charge.

This phase is steeped in partnership building and publicizing the project. Partnerships are key to reach the objectives of community building and building awareness of the cultural assets in the community.

The dollmaking and quilting class were conducted simultaneously. Initially we tried to close the sliding wall between the two classrooms, but after the first session, the divider remained open and the space was transformed into a folklife orchestra. When the dollmaking class concluded, storytelling began while the quilting class continued. The interchange between the children and the adults, the stories and the needles, melded like a harmonic symphony. Within a sociocultural framework, young children learned as apprentices alongside more experienced members of the culture. When a quilter heard the activities in the storytelling class, she encouraged six of her grandchildren to enroll. The total attendees for the storytelling class eventually rose to 10. Storytelling was also integral to the dollmaking and quilting classes. While wearing multiple hats—administrator, recorder, storyteller, cultural ambassador—I asked questions to stimulate the telling of stories and discussion of community issues.

We held an intergenerational lunch during midsession. The conversation continually circled back to the importance of building relationships. The decision was to create social art that addressed the need to deepen the relationships in our community. When friendship was identified as the vehicle to address the root of community's sociocultural issues, the more experienced quilters were excited to share the history and patterns of code quilts. The adults in the group started telling stories about how friendship was a fundamental element during the enslavement period and how it was important in planning escapes on the Underground Railroad. "Traditional stories or personal stories of life experiences allow elders to communicate history, knowledge and wisdom to youth in ways that youth might not otherwise countenance" (Rankin, Hansteen-Izora, and Packer 2006).

Teaching artist Winnie Thomas said, "We should use the Bear's Paw in the joint project!" The Bear's Paw pattern was also called the Hand of Friendship by the Quakers. Hanging on a fence of a friend of the Underground Railroad, it sent the message that it was time to take the tracks north through the woods. As the conversation progressed, nine-year-old Jordan chimed in, "We should add a heart." The decision was made to create a quilt with the Bear's Paw pattern, imprints of the children's hands, a heart, and a square that represented each workshop class. The project in its totality symbolized intergenerational friendship; a connection across artistic disciplines; and the connection to knowing your history as force to move forward.

Stories continued to permeate the remaining Saturday sessions as the students quilted and made dolls. We heard family historical tales, personal stories that spoke to the need to instill old values in today's world, and hair stories from adults and youth that addressed issues of identity in the African American community. The storytelling sessions followed up on the history of code quilts. The children learned to tell a coded message that seemed to be talking about rabbits and cabbages but was actually a traditional call and response sung by African Americans to warn that it was time to escape.

The registrations for the hip hop and the blues were slow to emerge, so Kendall suggested we put it inside of the Youth Teen Workshop that was already in place by the Recreation Department. Flexibility and the ability to seize opportunity were crucial to the success of the project, as there were variants that altered the original plans. Hip hop and the blues was a perfect match with the Teen Program and the open space of the quilting, dollmaking, and storytelling workshops developed into the intergenerational creative placemaking space envisioned during the planning stages.

Hip Hop and the Blues Story

Three weeks before the tragedy of Sandy Hook, Sarai introduced her students to "Little Weapon" by Lupe Fiasco. This hip-hop piece poignantly looks at the destruction of childhood through the lens of children with guns, from child soldiers, to high school shooters to violent video games.

After hearing and reading the lyrics, students were engaged in the following discussion:

- Analyze a hip-hop piece in its musical context: Lupe Fiasco's "Little Weapon."
- Analyze the same piece from a literary point of view: words inform and speak thought to action—what are they saying? What are they asking?
- Discuss implications: Who are child soldiers? Where are child soldiers? What is the American presence of child soldiers?
- Examine feelings: How would you feel being held hostage? What would you do in the context of those feelings?
- Journal: Write a story. How did the child soldier/hostage taker get to that point? What is he feeling? What is he thinking?
- Share written works using the prompt: He had a gun in his hand...

The ensuing discussion was rich and the sharing was abundant and amazing! In response, the 14-year-old student artists embodied reflective responses. Two are partially quoted:

He had a gun in his right hand cocked to the side unlike a real man. Sweat dripping down his brow. Time stops. I remember seeing him last night on the streets crying out for help from anyone that would listen. . . . He's point the gun at himself saying I'm sorry. He says for all the wrong. Every woman I touched, every baby & mother I've dropped in cold blood, every father I've taken. He ain't never had that. The gun still in his right hand but pointed at his head.

> *He had a gun in his hand. When that kid said his mom didn't love him, they didn't know his mom left when he was three.*
> *They punched him day after day ... they didn't know his Dad abuses him when he comes home drunk.*
> *They called him stupid, they didn't know he had dyslexia.*
> *They made fun of his clothes, they didn't know their electricity, water, and heat had been turned off. He was sick of it and wanted pay back for making his life miserable. They called him weak ... They didn't know this would be how he found dominance.*

One program counselor spoke with amazement and gratitude, "We have had been trying to get our teens to write for weeks. This is the first time they wrote past three sentences—and with depth and critical thought!"

Dr. Caroliese Frink Reed, African oral tradition scholar, avers that "Blackstorytelling" maintains a premise that spirit is never separate from *Jaliya* (the Art of Storytelling). Predisposing this topic to middle-school children, just three weeks prior to the national tragedy of Sandy Hook infiltrating every home in America, confers the underpinnings of spirit and universal connectedness.

Phase III—Exhibition and Concert

The workshops are scheduled to end with an exhibition and concert. Instead of creating a new event, the planning committee folded the conclusion of the workshop series into the Annual Willingboro Kwanzaa Fest that

Mounting a quilting display

already has a built-in audience of nearly 300. This results in increased awareness of the project, deepens conversations of social issues through the artwork, and increases partnership alliances and individual interests.

The 2012 exhibition included a display of 30 quilts, seven of which were made during Family & Folklife. The dollmaking class displayed eight dolls. All master artists conducted workshops at the final event, and the storytelling students performed.

Phase IV—Evaluation and Assessment

To test the assumptions in our social impact theory, we gather quantitative and qualitative data. In addition to using questionnaires, focus groups, unobstructed observation, interviews, and artists' debriefing are held.

The methods are used to determine if need was identified or impact made; obtain feedback from the participants; make midcourse adjustments; determine what actions can be taken based on the findings; analyze how the community can be better served; and, consider what else is possible and how can it get better than this.

Outtakes from 2012 Artists' Debriefing

Alma Day, dollmaking, wrote:

> *The children's interests were peaked, especially when they were stuffing their dolls. It appeared that a personality was being born. My high moment was to see the innocent, raw joy of the faces of Jordan and Iasia when they actually sewed on the machine for the very first time, as I taught them the basic parts. As I tread in this virgin place/field that held no obstacles—only a story, I felt the power in empowering other through my talents. The children unleashed stories they never told. They spoke to their dolls, held their arms so they did a jig on the sewing table, made fashion decisions, and finally at the round table conducive to these Masters of creations, they chose a fitting name for their story—Flowers, Sally, and Power.*
>
> *The young man who wanted to make a Ninja doll face lit-up when he grasped that power did not exist in just fighting. We worked with his doll to show that fathers are good leaders and nurturers and that there can be a compromise between ninja and gentle. We incorporated what he needed and what he wanted. I learned that the teacher's interaction in this environment strengthens values of children.*

Sarai Abdul-Malik, hip hop and the blues, shared, "When the teens engaged in a new musical genre, it expanded their worldviews. The workshop format that included storytelling and an introduction to writing blues and Hip Hop formats expanded the participants' intellectual and cultural amplitude. Students' intellectual repertoire was built through the constructing of ideas, and making connections to current issues."

Audience

The workshop target audience for Burlington County residents varied in accordance with the discipline. The dollmaking and quilting were

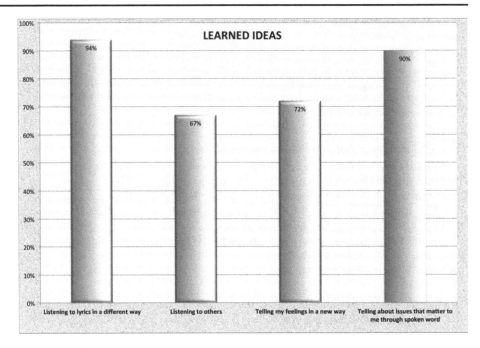

Learned Ideas

intergenerational from ages nine to eldership. Storytelling was for youth ages nine and up. Hip hop and the blues had teen attendance. The concert and exhibition targeted family audiences and a broader regional geographic area.

Funding

The initial project was funded by the National Storytelling Network's Brimstone Grant for $5,000, a Target Gift Card to purchase sewing machines, and other partners. In FACT has received a grant from the Burlington County Board of Freeholders for the past three years to support the project, in addition to growing contributions by partners and vending fees for the final event.

Community Collaborators

The community partners are given key recognition at the final event, The Annual Willingboro Kwanzaa Festival, with tables to display their organization's work and impact.

Partnerships include the Township of Willingboro, Rancocas Valley Alumnae Chapter of Delta Sigma Theta Inc., Keepers of the Culture Inc. (Philadelphia's Afrocentric Storytelling Group), I am Kenny J Productions, Willingboro Garden Association, Zeta Delta Zeta Chapter of Zeta Phi Beta Sorority Inc., Jack and Jill of Burlington County, the Underground Railroad of Burlington County, the Nation of Islam Willingboro Study Group, and B.O.Y.D.

Successive Years

The 44 workshop evaluations and 55 surveys collected from the final event provided a larger research sampling and greatly increased community involvement in the research process. Nineteen of the 52 surveyed previously knew about the Family, Fun & Folklife Workshop series, and 87 percent of the respondents indicated that they are interested in some type of folk art classes and events. The survey questions attempted to assess contemporary thought on the role of folk art, culture, and tradition as well the community's opinions about the most pressing issues on the local, national, and global levels. The results have aided in successive year planning.

How-to Guide

My *Artist as Community Cultural Ambassador How-To-Guide* is designed like a story, beginning, middle, and end, and includes worksheets and guides to develop the following: Artist Statement, The Need, Location and Demographics, Field Notes, Partnerships, Target Audience; Program Designed, Budget, Communications Plan, Documentation, Assessment, and Surveys.

(Publication forthcoming, in the meantime feel free to reach me at e-mail: infactorg@gmail.com. Websites: www.queennur.com; www.innovativefact.org.)

Bibliography

Black Storytellers Speak. Directed by Oni Lasana at the National Association of Black Storytelling Conference, Rochester, NY. Digital videotape, Philadelphia: Keepers of the Culture, 2000.

Dees, J. Gregory, Jed Emerson, and Peter Economy. *Enterprising Nonprofits: A Toolkit for Social Entrepreneurs.* New York: John Wiley & Sons, Inc., 2001.

Fiasco, Lupe. "Little Weapon." *The Cool.* CD. Atlantic Records, 2007. https://play.google.com/music/preview/Tcj6g5a3qn65engg5t7lb26bf74?lyrics=1&utm_source=google&utm_medium=search&utm_campaign=lyrics&pcampaignid=kp-lyrics (the lyrics); https://youtu.be/yvHGPVNSwnU?list=PLjiR_cIfafMJZnKphFc1NRJcakPHchRiN (the video).

Fiske, Edward, ed. *Champions of Change: The Impact of the Arts on Learning*, the Arts Education Partnership, the President's Committee on the Arts and the Humanities, 1999, website accessed October 2011, http://artsedge.kennedy-center.org/champions/pdfs/ChampsReport.pdf.

Langellier, Kristin, and Eric Peterson. *Storytelling in Daily Life: Performing Narrative.* Philadelphia: Temple University Press, 2004.

Light, Paul. *The Search for Social Entrepreneurship.* Washington, DC: Brookings Institution Press, 2008.

Rankin, Paul, Robin Hansteen-Izora, and Lara Packer. *"Living Cultural Storybases": Self-Empowering Narratives for Minority Cultures.* Peer-reviewed paper for the International Community Informatics Conference on "Constructing and Sharing Memory: Community Informatics, Identity, and Empowerment," CIRN Prato Italy, October 9–11, 2006.

Shiponi, Limor, "Storytelling Genres: Applied Storytelling," January 10, 2011, http://www.limorshiponi.com/2011/01/10/storytelling-genres-applied-storytelling/.

Additional Readings

Abdul-Malik, Karen. *What Is the Role of Storytelling in Cultural Sustainability? Four Case Studies.* Report submitted for Capstone

Requirement for the degree of masters of arts in cultural sustainability. Townsend, MD: Goucher College, 2012.

Borrup, Tom. *The Creative Community Builder's Handbook: How to Transform Communities Using Local Assets, Art, and Culture.* Saint Paul, MN: Fieldstone Publishing Center, 2006.

Cox, Allison, and David H. Albert, eds. *The Healing Heart and Communities: Stories to Build Strong and Healthy Communities.* Gabriola Island, Canada: New Society Publishers, 2003.

Markusen, Ann, and Anne Gadwa. *Creative Placemaking.* A White Paper for the Mayor's Institute on City Design, a leadership initiative of the National Endowment for the Arts in partnership with the U.S. Conference of Mayors and American Architectural Foundation, Washington, DC, 2010. Website accessed September 2015, https://www.arts.gov/sites/default/files/CreativePlacemaking-Paper.pdf.

National Park Service. *NPS-28 Cultural Resource Management Guidelines,* website accessed November 2012, https://www.nps.gov/parkhistory/online_books/nps28/28intro.htm.

Reed, Caroliese Frink, "Our Legacy, Our Lineage, Our Love," *Storytelling Magazine,* September/October 2007, 40.

Sarkissian, Wendy. *Kitchen Table Sustainability: Practical Recipes for Community Engagement with Sustainability.* Abingdon, United Kingdom: Routledge, 2008.

Skillman, Amy E. "For Safe Keeping: The Power of Artistic Traditions," November 2010, www.folkartpa.org/essays.html.

Solinger, Rickie, Madeline Fox, and Kyhan Irani, eds. *Telling Stories to Change the World: Global Voices on the Power of Narrative to Build Community and Make Social Justice Claims.* New York: Routledge, 2008.

Becoming Visible through Our Stories

Nancy Wang

So often, Asians have been described as the *invisible minority*. We have also been described as *inscrutable, nerds, exotic, good at math, wimpy, docile, our men un-masculine, our women dragon ladies or the opposite—subservient.* The latest accusation is that we are *trying to take over the world*!

But, if you know any Asians or Asian Americans, what would you say about us? If you do not know any Asians, then you might be prone to believe those stereotypes.

Enter Eth-Noh-Tec, storytellers Nancy Wang and Robert Kikuchi-Yngojo, whose goals are to break up those stereotypes with ancient folktales and myths as well as with inspiring contemporary Asian American stories. Eth-Noh-Tec's mission is to create art that heals the divides within us and between us.

Whenever we perform, the multicultural audiences experience the universality of the values inherent in our stories, and thus, cultural bridges are built and stereotypes disrupted. In this way, our mission to create art that heals the divides within us and between us is delivered.

In addition, we produce events that will deepen and engage the public in their own sense of identity and their respect for others. We do this through researching their own stories, their histories, art, panel discussions, workshops, special events (e.g., Asian American Story Festival, cross-cultural multidisciplinary art salons, tours to Asia), apprenticeship programs, and most recently books.

Why? Why do we spend all our time and energy on delivering programs that will help this country become more savvy about all of its citizens? As persons of color, we are very aware of the blind nature of the average Americans. We often explain it with "does a fish know it is swimming in water?"

Growing up Asian, or for any ethnic group other than European, we as Americans have all experienced the same response from Euro Americans. They ask (enunciating each word as if we do not understand), "Where. Were. You. Born?" "You. Speak. Such. Good. English! No. Accent!" "How. Long. Have. You. Been. Living. In. The. United. States?" "Welcome. To. My. Country." I can be walking down the street or sitting at a café or at a party with a friend from France or Sweden or Germany or England, and I will be the one assumed to be the foreigner. On my mother's side, I am a fifth-generation American! We have been in this country since 1850.

Why does this continue to happen? Why have white Americans not changed the way they see us—or see us at all? I have had people say to me, "You aren't Chinese to me. I don't see you as different than me." Meaning? I am as white as she is? This is a double message: one is positively seeing me as just as human as she is, while the other denies my rich cultural heritage as Chinese. Why do Asians remain so invisible?

Well, for one, most of the stars and characters in America's television shows, print media, and movies continue to be white and black. Go around the world, and the way people see Americans are as blonde and blue-eyed, or black. The first time I went to China and visited my father's family, one aunt-in-law asked if I were the American relative, why did not I have blond hair and blue eyes?

More recently, the inaugural speech of President Obama spoke about America as a white, black, and brown nation, leaving out the yellow and red. Listening to a recent keynote speech at a conference, the speaker's examples of excellence were mostly white and a few blacks despite the fact that the speaker had examples of brown and yellow students who had also excelled in theater arts. After speaking with him about this, he said he simply had not thought about it! Another storytelling author sent me the index of the stories she was including in her book of stories from around the world. The stories originated only from the varied European countries.

Are we that invisible? Does a fish know it is in water?

These behaviors by the mainstream perpetuate people of color being cast to the edges, kept out of the centers of circles where they can contribute. At the same time, all Americans are cheated of an enriching and more worldly experience in which to grow when such separations and exclusions are the norm. From our experiences, Eth-Noh-Tec has a very strong motive, both personally and collectively, to help create a more inclusive society and has found that the best way to do this is through stories, art, and dialogue. That is what we do.

Folktales and Myths

The reason why folktales and myths have lasted for over a thousand years is because there is an intrinsic value embedded in them that every society must embrace in order to live a good life. So when choosing a folktale or myth from your own ethnic group or culture, look for the message. Choose the values, the messages that resonate with what you find important and what is needed in society. Libraries and bookstores will have a section labeled "Folklore and Mythology." Read as many as you can. You will find and clarify what speaks to your heart.

Personal Stories

Eth-Noh-Tec loves personal stories, but only if, like a folktale or myth, it has something important to share about living a life of quality and meaning. So when looking at your own life, or the life of others, make sure you are choosing a story that has the potential of making a difference in another's life. For example, among our personal stories, we interviewed an atom bomb survivor and wrote the story, "Takashi's Dream," about his journey from rage and revenge to forgiveness and reconciliation. Another is the story, "Red Altar," about six teens who traveled in 1850 on a junk boat from China and started the fishing industry in Monterey, California, during decades of anti-Chinese legal and illegal violence. It is a story about generations of Chinese whose skills, persistence, ingenuity, and courage helped to build America and its economy despite the racism. In the end, this story connects to the legal and illegal violence against people of color still here in America.

History

The same guidelines are used to tell an important part of history, especially one that has not been heard before and needs to be heard to demonstrate that America was not just made of European settlers. A common historic event can also be told from a different, more rounded perspective other than that written by only one culture or ethnic group. The value of diversity is a focus here. Inclusivity is a focus here. The more we all understand and have knowledge that many ethnic groups have contributed to the making of America, the more we will embrace each other as Americans rather than seeing suspiciously or as not belonging. This kind of belief leads to dissonance and even violence. It leads to thinking in terms of us versus them, mine and not yours.

Art

There are many ways to make art both creative and meaningful. Collage is a very easy way to get people involved with art. You do not need to be a painter or calligrapher or someone who knows how to draw. Art can be intimidating for many of us. So make it easy so people can concentrate on creating what is in their mind and heart. For meaning, use a theme such as immigration. We held a day of art after hearing stories of non-Western names, an excerpt from our "Red Altar" immigration piece, and a panel on immigration. Not only did participants make art on the theme of either their own immigration or on the ancestor who first immigrated, but we also organized a photo essay component in which individuals were photographed with their artwork and spoke about the immigrant in their family: who immigrated, why did that family member immigrate, from where and when, and finally how that person contributed to the life of the individual. There are many themes to focus on—even on an aspect of the stories participants are working on. We provide all the art supplies: paperboards that stationary stores will throw out; trinkets from Goodwill or Salvation Army—any free giveaway places as well as secondhand stores; magazines such as *National Geographic*; old calendars; and pens, paints and paint brushes, scissors, markers, colored pencils, tape, glue, and hot glue gun—all there to inspire. Friends with grown-up kids might still have lots of these left over to donate. People can fill hours and hours doing their art, and when they are done, they share their work and the meaning in it. It is fun and relaxing and all the while creates a sense of community at each table and as the group as a whole. Many discussions evolve out of the shares.

Panel Discussions

Panels are a great way to learn about each other, about a topic, or about a culture. Not only do you get to hear differing perspectives on the same subject, but there is always a time provided for a Q&A in which more can be learned and understood. There are many people in one's community who are experts and passionate about something that also interests you and that you feel would be a positive addition to a performance or event. Most people are honored to be asked and will not need to be paid. People do not just like to be heard; they need to be heard, to be part of a community that is interested in the same things. As mentioned before, we organized a panel on immigration with people who work with immigrants along with people who are illegal immigrants or their parents are. Having heard their stories, audiences leave with far more empathy and understanding. We have also had a panel with Asian American storytellers talking about why they do what they do. Everyone is enlightened and communities are enhanced. Inclusivity increases, barriers are removed, and bridges are built.

Workshops

Eth-Noh-Tec has several workshops: Asian Pacific Playshop: a hands-on experience with Asian music instruments, songs, and dances, sharing Asian culture through its art forms; Identity and Beyond: understanding the difference between Eastern and Western philosophy and sociology and how it applies to the way we are in the world and the importance to not judge or interpret our own behaviors through the lens of the other; and Tell It with Movement and More: to help others enhance their telling with movement and gesture so that their storytelling is more effective and therefore more impactful. Again, if we experience and understand each other's culture, there is less prejudice and less distrust of each other. We are building bridges that are fun and informative at the same time!

Special Events

Eth-Noh-Tec has produced several events that present Asian storytellers all on one stage at one time, each different than the other in art form, style, and certainly physicality. We have all been mistaken for the other Asian teller by non-Asians who have a hard time differentiating our faces. The saying that we all look the same seems to be quite alive! Why? Maybe, for example, in national storytelling festivals around the country or in Europe, only 1 Asian act is among 4–15 Euro American performers. One gets to see that Euro Americans differ one from the other, but that is not the opportunity for Asians. This kind of continuing stab at "diversity" with one Asian, or one Latina, or one African American, or one Native teller or performer among the many Euro Americans only confirms our marginality and does not provide the opportunity to break the stereotype that we all look alike. It perpetuates the belief that we are one-dimensional. We might as well, in fact, be invisible. We also present multicultural salons with varied ethnic groups. This kind of cross-fertilization allows for the development of a truly multicultural community, while the varied art forms allow for the cross-fertilization of audiences. Again, inclusivity, the breaking up of stereotypes, and enriching everyone's lives with the true nature of our world are the goals. We provide the opportunity to remove oneself from the Eurocentric belief that the world is majority European and European power. This also works for our tours to Asia. American storytellers of all ethnic groups experience storytellers of China or India and share our many stories with each other. They then walk away with a realistic view of the peoples and their culture rather than the stereotypes spun by movies and the media. I cannot encourage you enough to provide this kind of opportunity and experience for your constituents! It will help to save our humanity. Truth is a vital ingredient for peace.

Apprenticeship Program

For at least a decade now, Eth-Noh-Tec has been auditioning and training Asian performing artists in the art of storytelling. We have been training them in our particular kinetic style of telling that uses gesture, highly choreographed stylized movement, and the rhythmic musical use of the spoken words. This is our way of continuing the important contributions of Asian cultures and of course our goals to build bridges between peoples and our mission to heal the divides. Again, storytelling is effective because it reaches the hearts and minds of all ages. Lectures and classes on Asian culture are important, but stories are not just for the mind and the intellect, but for the heart. The heart is where we will make a difference in our healing with each other.

Books

We have most recently launched into writing books. *A New Pair of Wings* (Parkhurst Brothers Publishers, 2016) is our new illustrated children's book on Robert's mom's immigration to San Francisco when she was five years old and how she managed to overcome the ridicule and language barrier. It is a story of persistence and magic! The other upcoming book will tell the "Red Altar" story—another story of persistence and courage that immigrants must have in order to make a life in America and thrive despite the racism. These books hope to not only bolster recent immigrants but also create a more compassionate society about newcomers to any land. After all, at some time in each of our histories, someone was an immigrant. It is very important to make that distinction. If we are to continue as a race, we must not perpetuate the destructive thinking of *us versus them*.

You may now be thinking these are all noble deeds and ideas; but how do I fund them? If you are smarter than we are, you will think ahead and apply for grants! There are many grants available for this sort of work, both with your local state arts council and private foundations and with the national funders such as the National Endowment for the Arts or the National Endowment for the Humanities if you are an educational institution.

However, we were not always that organized to think a year ahead to write a grant for a project a year or more away. But, we are creative thinkers and we have many in our communities who will volunteer if asked—artists, photographers, performers, activists. If your project is exciting and topical, there will be many who want to be a part of it. And then there is also the door—ticket sales. While we are lucky to have our own space, spaces such as church basements, social halls, the YWCA, or a friend's dance studio can go for very little or for nothing. Again, if your project is exciting and meaningful, even these spaces will want to be a part of it. Never underestimate just asking!

And so in closing, I have one thing to say: Step out there! Become visible! Bask in the knowledge that you matter. Learn your stories and share them in many unique ways. There is not just one way. You do not have to be a performing storytelling star! You have your own way of making a difference. Believe in it. Become visible with pride!

I know that was more than one thing to say!

Building Community through Cultural Storytelling

Rose McGee

I am not a chicken, but an eagle!
I Am Not a Chicken, But an Eagle!
I AM NOT A CHICKEN, BUT AN EAGLE!
Years ago, those words were a mantra for our Arts-Us Young Storytellers of Saint Paul, Minnesota. The youth, ages eight and up, would chant the phrase at the start of rehearsals and often as they prepared for storytelling performances. In storytelling, the act of *trebling* or repeating a statement three times emphasizes the truth and consequence of a matter. When spoken the first time, Mouth whispers to Brain saying, *May I have your attention please*? When repeated the second time, Brain wakes up Heart by proclaiming, *I Understand! Can You Feel It*? Keenly alert by the third time, Heart rhythmically *responds* to Brain's vibrant *call* with a confident *Yes! I got this!*

For almost 10 years, I coached this talented group of youth who were in every sense of the word—the best storytellers ever. In 1997, the Arts-Us Young Storytellers were the first youth group to perform in the National Association of Black Storytellers Festival held in Philadelphia, which then inspired other cities to form youth storytelling groups. They presented nationally, including a special visit in 1999 to the Panafest International Storytelling Festival in Ghana, West Africa.

The repertoire of stories acquired by these youth was of wide span. Just as they eagerly retold stories heard from legendary African American storytellers such as Elder Nothando Zulu, Mother Mary Carter Smith, Linda Goss, Valada Parker Flewellyn, W. Toni Carter, Brother Blue, Jerry Blue, Tejumola Ologboni, and Vusi Zulu, they also captured classic stories from books such as *Talk That Talk* (Goss and Barnes 1989), an anthology of stories told by black storytellers, and *The Frog Who Wanted to Be a Singer* (Goss 1996). Several created and developed their own stories and poetry that became group stories that incorporated the ensemble. The core team was comprised of 8–10 youth who were all inner-city, majority African American, and several with academic challenges in school. There was an additional group of youth who were unable to fulfill the time commitment of tours or artist-in-residency programs but were available to attend our summer workshops or presented during local events.

Black parents also want the best for their children!
Black Parents Also Want the Best for Their Children!
BLACK PARENTS ALSO WANT THE BEST FOR THEIR CHILDREN!
When considering the question—*which came first in making this group such a sensational wow factor—the chicken or the eagle egg?*—like most of us educators, the founder of the Arts-Us organization, W. Toni Carter, recognized early on the power of the oral tradition and its positive impact toward student learning. We also understood the value of making this engaging art form relevant not only to the youth but to assist the parents as well. We recognized the challenges often associated with parent involvement, so we intentionally respected each family's personal situation and level of commitment.

There is such a misconception that black parents are not concerned about the well-being of their children. Nothing is so far from the truth. Several parents brought their children into our program because they wanted an outlet that allowed the youth to be expressive. There were others who simply wanted a safe place for their children to hang out. Although our program provided both, what surfaced as a key inspiration for each child wanting to remain with the program were the relationships created among the adult leaders and their peers. As a result, the youth learned countless stories, did their absolute best, and always showed up. However, we never forgot a key ingredient—these youths were there in the first place because of their parents. Were there times when parents were late picking a child up from rehearsal? Yes. Were there times when my minivan became the taxi for several of the youth when parents were not available to transport their children to various events or performances? Yes. Things happen; we understood, and we moved on without penalties and judgment. As a result, parents gained a strong sense of trust for and with us. They became volunteer chaperones, provided snacks, and were always our greatest community allies.

Respectfully, the youth grew in relationship with us (the adult leaders) and with their peers. Here is what is critical: not only did they want to model stories told by elders, but they also wanted to *be like* their peers who demonstrated good storytelling. I remember how young Melvin Carter III (our first Arts-Us Young Storyteller who at the time was in high school) would tell with incredible animation what became his signature story, "Signifying Monkey." My son, Adam Davis-McGee (who was in elementary school at the time), would be totally mesmerized whenever Melvin performed that story. A couple of years later, when Melvin went off to Florida A&M University, Adam stepped in and began telling "Signifying Monkey." Although he added his own spin to the tale, clearly he used some of Melvin's exact moves and verbal iterations. It was great! Soon when other younger tellers joined the group, they watched Adam and would mimic him, although actually much of it was Melvin twice removed.

When I learned about the Gullah people (West Africans held as slaves off the Carolinas and Georgia coasts), I became intrigued by the history of their survival. During the Civil War, many of their white owners fled and left the captives to fend for themselves on those beautiful barrier islands. After the war ended, the U.S. government granted the land to those black residents. Being free now and in isolation, the residents were able to maintain many of their African traditions—the food, the basket weaving, and so on. Keep in mind, these were people from many different nations who had been forced to speak English. As a result of an array of interpretations, they created their own dialect and later became known as the Gullah or Geechee people.

In my opinion, the Gullah culture represents the indigenous blacks in this country. I wanted the young storytellers to know this hidden treasure that resides in America's history. Well, little Miss Brianna Lark sure took me seriously. She listened to all my CDs of songs that featured the infamous Georgia Sea Island Singers and Gullah storyteller, Aunt Polly Sue. Before I knew it, Brianna was speaking the Gullah dialect as though she came straight from one of the islands. Audiences loved listening to her stories. Her father said to me once in a half-teasing manner, "You are un-training my daughter of what's taken years for her to learn...proper English!"

On the other hand, not all of the young storytellers were as quick to learn stories and tell with such animation as others. I remember Joslyn who was shy, yet she received the greatest thrill just being with the storytelling troupe. Although she was not a great teller, she was always improving on her own ability, which made her great. One day her grandmother said to me, "Joslyn's teacher asked me what in the world was she doing these days because her ability to share in class had really changed. She's become more engaged, her homework is getting done, and her grades have improved significantly. I told her it was because of the storytelling group. I want to thank Arts-Us for what you all have done for my granddaughter." She was in tears.

The youth referenced previously are all grown up now. Brianna passed away in 2011 from health complications at age 21. Most are now in their late 20s and 30s. Some now are parents with children who are older than they were when they first became members of the storytelling troupe. Often I hear, "Mrs. McGee, when are you going to start storytelling again so my child will have the same wonderful opportunity that I had?" Others have said, "If it hadn't been for storytelling when I was growing up, I wouldn't be doing the job that I love now." One who lives in California now and is in acting stated, "The storytelling and acting opportunities that I learned during my time with you really did save my life." Now that she is all grown up with two active little storytellers of her own, I am proud that Alanna Carter Galloway is responding to the call of coaching storytelling to youth in the community.

Nowadays, I spend my core time helping educators understand the power of story. As an educator, a story circle facilitator, and a professional storyteller, I want teachers and community educators to understand the motivation that inspires student achievement. When students are given a chance to share (with pride) who they are in their schools and in the classrooms and see *themselves* reflected in curriculum, *all* students can grow into a relationship with their teacher and vice versa. My theoretical equation for this occurrence is as follows:

WHAT: *Genuine Interest in Students* × *Listening* = *Relationship Building*
WHO: *Teachers* + *Students* + *Parents* = *Academic Success*
HOW: *Invite Parents* × *Story Circles–Stereotyping* = *Cultural Intelligence*

When parents are *invited* into the classroom and into the world of their children, all students are able to acquire deeper understanding of the positive and rich aspects of diversity. Being in Minnesota, I often present in small communities that have only white residents. During a storytelling residency in one such town, the elementary school's population was 225 with only 4 students of color—2 adopted African-born and two Chinese. My work was with fourth graders. An assignment for the students was: "Tell a story about who you are." I left it open for them to be as creative as possible.

On the day of sharing their stories, a grandfather was in attendance. I thought, *how cool, the Grandpa is here*. The Grandpa sat through each student's presentation while exhibiting tremendous interest. When they were all done, I asked him if he had any comments to share with the class. Enthusiastically, he stated, "The real reason that I'm here today is because nobody ever asked me about who I am or who my family is. I wanted to hear the stories from the kids." He was in tears.

The white Grandpa made me realize the importance of *all* voices. Students learn from each other. Parents learn from each other. Assumptions are often made based upon perceived ideals regarding one cultural group or the other. To hear this man say that he was in the classroom to *learn* from a group of fourth graders because of what he never received was powerful and eye-opening for me. Storytelling is a key bridge to closing relationship gaps.

My master's degree from Leslie University in Cambridge, Massachusetts, is in Creative Arts in Learning, with specialization in incorporating the arts into curriculum. It actually sounds like a mouthful as one tries to grasp the total concept. There is disaster when educators continue following the *normal* archaic rule of standardized thumb (a thumb is already short; should have nubbed itself down to being out of existence by now). Teachers must apply creativity as they establish relevant curriculum that will inspire all students. Nationally, budgets continue to hack away at the arts. So how then will children learn about humanity? How will children understand the process of tapping inside themselves and discovering their own positive potential? Storytelling and the arts can be integrated into science and math just as effectively as they are used in English and history. My role is to help educators realize the pedagogical possibilities when storytelling is woven into the mix.

As an Arts-Us Young Storyteller, Anthony Galloway, who as an adult now leads school districts in racial equity, created a story called "Bubba and the Boogie Man."

Bubba and the Boogie Man

Anthony Galloway

Bubba was a little boy whose father was a preacher. One night when Bubba was finishing up his outdoor chores and was heading back inside the house, out jumped the Boogie Man. Three times, he attempted to scare Bubba to death. The first time he jumped out at Bubba and said, "Bubba, I'm gonna rip you to shreds!"

Bubba could feel that Boogie Man's hot breath trailing down the back of his neck. Somehow, though, Bubba found a little voice inside himself and began to imitate his southern Black Baptist Preacher, "I ain't scared of you, Boogie Man. You'd better go on and leave me alone." Although trembling profusely, Bubba kept on walking. The surprise of Bubba's verbal response caused the Boogie Man to step back. After all, he was expecting the kid to take off running in fear.

"Bubba, I don't think you heard me: I'm gonna take you and toss you off that high cliff and let the buzzards come and eat you alive!"

Bubba noticed that the Boogie Man was no longer breathing down the back of his neck—not as close upon him at all. So he gained a bit more confidence in his voice and spoke up louder (but kept on walking). "I don't care what you say, Boogie Man. I told you already that I ain't scared of you. Best you go on back where you came from!" (Still shaking, Bubba kept on walking).

Totally taken off guard now, the Boogie Man, stepped back even further, but called out to Bubba again, "Bubba! This time I tell you what...in just a few minutes, I'm gonna show you who's the boss, cause I'm gonna snatch you up and swallow you down my throat!"

Bubba noticed that the Boogie Man's voice was further and further away than before and that he (Bubba) was almost at the front door of his house. Feeling most confident now, Bubba reached down

*and pulled out his bass voice and shouted, "BOOGIE MAN! Don't
you know by now I ain't scared of you! I have told you once, I have
told you twice and now I'm telling you thrice. Stay ye behind me
and don't ever show your ugly self around me or my family again!
DO YOU HEAR ME!"*

*At this time, the Boogie Man jumped back, startled by Bubba's
booming voice, and took off into the night never to be heard from
by Bubba again. To this day Bubba still has no idea where his
booming voice evolved, but once he got inside the house, he fell on
his knees and prayed just like he'd heard his father, the preacher.
"Thank you Lord for saving me from that horrible Boogie Man,
cauz you know I sure was mighty scared! Amen."*

Anthony's story shows how he was able to craft a story based upon his
own heritage and family inspirations. Students should be allowed to bring
their stories into the classroom. Generally, Shakespearean or other
European works are used by teachers as models for students to then revise
into comparative contemporary versions. I submit to educators to begin using
the works of African Americans, Native Americans, Latinos, and other
diverse cultures. During a recent workshop that I facilitated, a white teacher
was (as she stated) ashamed to say, "I have no books in my classroom written
by black authors. I have no pictures on the walls of anyone other than whites.
I simply never thought about it until you are mentioning this now."

Well, that sure shocked the heck out of me at the time. Problem is that
was only in 2013. Again, it was one of those small Minnesota all-white towns.
Fortunately, when the workshop ended, that particular teacher, along with
others, committed to bringing visible diversity into the school and into their
classrooms. Sharing authentic stories can often settle aspects of ignorance.

Minnesota Humanities Center refers to missing voices as *absent narratives*. I like the term because it immediately catches one's attention. In reality, people who are traditionally marginalized really are not absent, yet a
systemic controlling factor devised out of power, greed, and fear has perpetuated invisibility to the extent of being outright obnoxious. Over 20 years ago,
I wrote a play, *Kumbayah—the Juneteenth Story*, which featured the Arts-Us
Young Storytellers along with community actors and musicians. The play is a
story within a story. The character of Frederick Douglass serves as *Narrator*,
while the youth tend to tell stories about the matters at hand. What made
each year's production so profound was listening to the cast interact with
audiences after each production.

*I never knew what Juneteenth was until I saw this play. This was
never taught to me in school.*

*How is it that people were able to be kept enslaved after President
Lincoln had freed the slaves? I don't understand how that could be.*

*Why is this play not produced in the community and in schools so
we know the truth about our history?*

Surprise! Those were comments from adults in the audience. Too often, I
address a room of educators and ask if they know what Juneteenth is, and,
depending on where I am, generally no hands go up at all. A few may have
heard of the celebration that goes on in the community but still do not know
the meaning. Although President Abraham Lincoln signed the

Emancipation Proclamation freeing the slaves in 1863, it was almost three years later before the captives in and around Texas got word of their freedom. When they did receive the news, it was on or around the June 19. Thus, the term *Juneteenth*. As we prepare for each rehearsal, the cast always convenes in a circle and responds to a prompt that gets us centered. The following is one that keeps me inspired:

Me:	Okay. Today, let's start with a simple prompt. Name one person that you admire most and why.
Youth:	My mom. She works hard to take care of us.
Another Youth:	My grandmother. She loves me a lot and gives me nice things.
Another Youth:	My teacher. She's really nice to me.
Another Youth:	Malcolm X. He was brave.
Another Youth:	You. You help me learn better.
Me:	(*Totally did not see that coming*; *pausing for composure, holding back tears*)
	Thank you.
	Thank You.
	THANK YOU!

Bibliography

Goss, Linda. *The Frog Who Wanted to be a Singer.* London, United Kingdom: Orchard Books, 1996.

Goss, Linda, and Marian E. Barnes, eds. *Talk That Talk: An Anthology of African-American Storytelling.* New York: Simon & Schuster, 1989.

4

Voices of Students
of All Ages

Education should not be the filling of a pail, but the lighting of a fire.
—William Butler Yeats

Editors' Comments

Storytelling lights a fire in students of all ages! In this chapter, you will learn about school-based, library-based, community-based, and college-based storytelling programs that bring student tellers to the stage.

Why?

The Partnership for 21st Century Learning lists the following traits among the most relevant, useful, in-demand, and universally applicable skills to meet the demands of the future:

- Critical thinking, problem solving, reasoning, analysis, interpretation, synthesizing information
- Research skills and practices, interrogative questioning
- Creativity, artistry, curiosity, imagination, innovation, personal expression
- Perseverance, self-direction, planning, self-discipline, adaptability, initiative
- Oral and written communication, public speaking and presenting, listening
- Leadership, teamwork, collaboration, cooperation

You will see all of these skills addressed within the storytelling projects described in this chapter.

But how do these storytelling projects engage community?

Easy! Storytelling is the art of communication, and communication is a noun of action: to share, impart, inform; and join, unite, participate in, literally to make common, from *communis.* Community is society, fellowship, friendly intercourse; courtesy, affability, from *communis. Munus* means the gift, and *cum* means together, among each other—literally to give gifts among each other.

Here are community storytelling opportunities in which students build communication skills, open the doors to understanding, and literally "give gifts among each other."

Creating Community through a College-Based Storytelling Program: The Storytelling Institute at South Mountain Community College

Liz Warren

Returning to teach for the Storytelling Institute would be a dream. Replicating their program in the Midwest would be a dream. My teaching changed. My life changed. My imagination changed. I am not the same person I was when I entered the program. When I tell others about the SMCC Storytelling Institute, they are amazed. What you have at South Mountain is a treasure.
                        —Storytelling certificate graduate (2014)

In 1994, a group of faculty and staff at South Mountain Community College in Phoenix, Arizona, were awakened to the power of oral, traditional storytelling as a pedagogy and as a vehicle for personal and professional growth and community engagement. The spark for that enlightenment came from Lorraine Calbow, a faculty member on our counseling staff, who became the first director of the SMCC Storytelling Institute.

Within a year, we had attended our first National Storytelling Network Conference, hosted Fall and Spring Storytelling Festivals, plunged into our own training as storytellers, and begun writing the curriculum that would become our 30-credit Academic Certificate in Storytelling. Twenty-plus years later, we have made storytelling a viable college discipline while simultaneously educating our community about the power and relevance of the art form.

We have one of the few, if not the only, academic programs in storytelling based at a community college. We would like to see that change. Storytelling can and should be available as a discipline at colleges and universities around the nation. The key elements to making that happen are a dedicated and well-trained storytelling faculty, a commitment to students and the community, quality programming, strong internal and external partnerships, and a commitment to diversity.

Committed Faculty Who Are Storytellers and a System That Supports Their Development

I think it would be great to offer more classes by, and overseen by, the great Storytelling Institute teachers not only at SMCC, but at the other Maricopa Community Colleges. Not just anyone can successfully teach a storytelling class. I think what is needed is great storytellers teaching the classes.
                        —Storytelling Certificate Graduate (2014)

To state it as plainly as possible, if you want a successful storytelling program, you need faculty who are passionate about the art of storytelling and who are storytellers themselves. This has been the key to our success. When Lorraine brought us together in 1994, we immediately saw the potential for a storytelling program, and we understood that we needed to be storytellers to make it happen. We embraced this because those of us who went on to be the core of the institute, all very much wanted to be storytellers. Lorraine Calbow describes that time:

> *During those early years, there was a steady core of seven people who kept the momentum with other key folks who ebbed and flowed back in as needed. All the individuals involved were established and mature career professionals. They were successful program planners, seasoned grant writers, key administrators of numerous innovative projects, master teachers and trainers, and proven educational as well as community and organizational leaders. The physical proximity of being at the same college strengthened and allowed the storytelling program to mushroom very quickly. Having a common vision and goal caused the SMCC Storytelling Institute to explode to producing two festivals a year, establishing a program of study, creating an interactive storytelling web site, and providing storytelling training and services to the community. We did this on top of our paid responsibilities.*

Jointly developing and achieving our storytelling goals, we became closer because we spent so much time together. We did storytelling training together. We practiced together. We performed together. We taught together. We planned together. We began to relate to each other differently. We learned to rely on one another's strengths, talents, and fits. We listened to each other's ideas and saw the value in incorporating and integrating each idea to strengthen our storytelling programs and events. More importantly, our love for storytelling allowed us to laugh and to have fun together" (Lorraine Calbow, "History of the SMCC Storytelling Institute," internal college document).

We went about developing the Storytelling Institute and pursuing our own training as storytellers very systematically. We held annual Fall and Spring Storytelling Festivals, and we chose local and national storytellers whom we knew would be a fit for our students and community and with whom we wanted to study. We went to the National Storytelling Conference every summer and to the National Storytelling Festival every October for several years. When the Mesa Storytelling Festival was established in 2004, we incorporated the tellers into our programming and faculty training.

Every storyteller we brought in made presentations to our classes, performed for students and our community, and delivered intensive training for our full-time and adjunct faculty. Over the years, we have featured storytellers who were excellent performers, skilled teachers, and represented both ethnic and stylistic diversity: Donald Davis, Don Doyle, Mary Gay Ducey, Doug Elliott, Elizabeth Ellis, Rex Ellis, Diane Ferlatte, Lyn Ford, Heather Forrest, Susan Klein, Michael Lacapa, Doug Lipman, Jim May, Margaret Read McDonald, Bobby Norfolk, Olga Loya, Jay O'Callahan, Connie Reagan-Blake, Antonio Rocha, Antonio Sacre, Jackie Torrance, Donna Washington, Liz Weir, and Emil Wolfgramm to name several. These tellers became our personal and professional guides and mentors. They shaped us as professional storytellers and as teachers of storytelling. We became storytellers.

Being part of a large, innovative, community college system has been crucial to our ability to establish, grow, and maintain a storytelling program. South Mountain Community College is part of the Maricopa Community

College District in metro Phoenix, Arizona. Maricopa is the largest community college district in the nation, and SMCC is the smallest and most diverse of its colleges. We leveraged the power of our college, our college district, and our personal and professional relationships to get the training we needed to create and grow a successful program.

Our chancellor at the time, Paul Elsner, gave us several thousand dollars in seed money to get the program going. Another colleague, Naomi Story, who directed the Maricopa Center for Learning and Instruction, also provided us with start-up funds. We used those funds to bring in the storytellers we wanted to work with for the first 10 years of the program. When those funds began to wane, our then college president, Ken Atwater, provided us with a small annual budget to support our programming. We supplement those funds with support from college partners such as the International/Intercultural Education program, Early College, Student Life, and the Maricopa American Indian Outreach.

We also took advantage of the professional growth funds we had access to as faculty. Those funds paid for our trips to conferences and festivals. We worked with our visiting storytellers to design the workshops we needed and then used funding from faculty professional growth to cover the fees. My colleague LynnAnn Wojciechowicz, who was the second director of the institute, received a sabbatical to develop curriculum on biographical storytelling. I was awarded two sabbaticals: the first to develop my repertoire and the second to complete the textbook that we use in our introductory course.

The college now supports two dedicated faculty positions in storytelling, the only ones in our community college district. Initially, LynnAnn Wojciechowicz and I had English positions. Overtime, as the storytelling classes continued to fill and succeed, we worked with the college and the district to rename the positions as storytelling. Similarly, originally the prefixes for our courses were ENG (English) and HUM (humanities). We worked with our district to create the STO prefix and to establish a Storytelling Instructional Council in parallel with all the other disciplines taught at our colleges. There are currently 45 STO prefix courses in the course bank, and the faculty at SMCC wrote them all.

Not every college or university has the resources that Maricopa does. In fact, Maricopa does not have the financial flexibility that it had in the 1990s. But all accredited institutions are mandated by their accrediting bodies to ensure that faculty has access to professional growth. People with passion can almost always find the resources needed to achieve their goals.

Faculty Training

As the number of storytelling classes has increased at South Mountain and around our district, so has the need for qualified full-time and adjunct faculty to teach them. Most college disciplines require a master's degree in the field or a set number of graduate credits in that discipline. Storytelling at the graduate level is rare, so we set the hiring qualifications to teach storytelling in our system very broadly. Those wishing to teach storytelling in our district must have a master's degree in any subject and have taken at least one 3-credit course in storytelling. Storytellers who have documented status or recognition in an indigenous, tribal, or religious context are also qualified to teach our beginning course.

Since our two basic courses, the Art of Storytelling and Multicultural Folktales, are cross-listed with English and humanities, faculty qualified to teach in either of those disciplines can teach them. That means that the courses are sometimes taught by people with no training in storytelling. This was a consequence we had to risk to make sure that we had a pool of faculty to teach the classes. Of the 20 people teaching storytelling in our district in the spring of 2016, 15 of them have taken some training with us at the Storytelling Institute. That training has included taking classes from the full-time storytelling faculty at SMCC and participating in workshops with us or the national-level storytellers we bring in, or in a week-long training we offer to Maricopa faculty who want to integrate storytelling into their curriculum.

My colleague, Marilyn Torres, the other full-time faculty member in the institute, has created a detailed curriculum guide for the Art of Storytelling. We ask those adjuncts who wish to teach for us at SMCC to first take the course from her and then to sit in on the class a second semester as they work through the curriculum and observe her teaching it. Five of our adjunct faculty have completed that training, and two more are currently in process. This results in adjuncts who are very well grounded in the course and its pedagogy and can teach for us or any of the other colleges in our system.

Student-Centered Curriculum with Artistic and Academic Integrity

> *The Storytelling Institute has been a joy to me. It hasn't been simply a place I've gone to take classes; it's been a fertile field of friendships and life-changing experiences that I'll never forget. The instructors have been more than just place holders and grade givers in a room. They have interacted with the students, encouraging, helping, supporting, training, and building confidence. In storytelling classes, the teachers remember not only your name, but your story.*
> —Storytelling Certificate Graduate (2014)

All the committed faculty in the world would not get far without courses that meet student needs. We have written courses that meet the needs of three groups of students: those pursuing their associate of arts degrees, committed storytelling students, and people from the community who have a particular need or focus.

Degree-Seeking Students

Our two foundational courses are the Art of Storytelling and Multicultural Folktales. They both meet two graduation requirements and transfer well to the university. This makes them very attractive to degree-seeking students.

Many students come to the Art of Storytelling on the first day expecting an easy humanities credit and that someone cozy will be reading to them. Imagine their surprise when they discover they will be doing the telling, both in and out of class, and that college-level reading and writing is expected. But for all the academic rigor of the class, it is still grounded in face-to-face, oral, traditional storytelling. Each student tells a folktale, a myth or legend, a fact-based story, and a personal story. They analyze 20 traditional stories from five culture areas, and they tell three times outside of class.

It is a beautiful thing to see students learn that they can be themselves, tell a story to others without memorizing, and be accepted and often celebrated for doing so. The bountiful capacity of storytelling to create community happens again and again in our basic storytelling classes. Twenty people from diverse social, economic, and ethnic backgrounds who might otherwise never have met form a caring community and friendships that last after the class ends as they watch each other learn and grow as storytellers. I think this may be the most important work that we do as a Storytelling Institute. It simultaneously changes people's lives and creates a deep awareness of storytelling as a viable, living art form in the community.

This semester, spring 2016, there are 20 Art of Storytelling classes being offered throughout Maricopa, serving about 400 students. We have been averaging 300–400 students in the Art of Storytelling across the district every fall and spring semester for the past several years, with a couple hundred more in the summer. That means that at least 1,000 people are having a significant college storytelling experience in the Phoenix metropolitan area every year. I believe this is part of the reason why Phoenix has such a vibrant storytelling scene. People in our area know what storytelling is and they like it.

Storytelling Certificate Students

The Art of Storytelling and Multicultural Folktales also serve as one of the entry points for our serious storytelling students who intend to complete the 30-credit Academic Certificate. The certificate consists of 18 hours of required courses and 12 hours of electives. The required courses are the following:

- **The Art of Storytelling:** In the introductory course, students tell a folktale, myth or legend, fact-based story, and a personal story. They also analyze world folktales, complete assigned readings, and tell outside of class.
- **Storytelling II:** This course focuses on repertoire and skill development and identity as a storytelling artist.
- **Multicultural Folktales:** The focus here is on folktales as a genre as students learn about traditional story structures, type and motif, and the persistent relevance of the folktale to modern culture.
- **Multicultural Folktales II:** Students in this class take a deep dive into one tale type and into the folktale tradition of a particular culture or region.
- **Using Storytelling in a Variety of Settings:** Students take this 3-credit class, or they can take three of the 1-credit setting classes that we offer: Using Storytelling in Business Settings, Education Settings, Advocacy Settings, Interpretive Settings, and Healing Settings.
- **Storytelling Practicum:** The practicum is a 60-hour capstone experience. Students must tell in public for a total of 15 hours. The other 45 hours are spent in planning, research, and reflection on their experience. The whole 60 hours are documented in a log and summarized in a final paper.

Certificate students can choose from a range of elective courses, including Creating and Telling Personal Stories, the Irish Storytelling Tradition, the African Storytelling Tradition, Telling Sacred Stories from around the World, Mythology, and Children's Literature.

By May 2017, 42 people will have completed the Academic Certificate in Storytelling. The majority of our certificate holders are females, in their middle years, who already have degrees and careers. While a few tell professionally, the majority have integrated the skills into their careers or use them in volunteer contexts.

The institute has begun partnering with other college and district programs to reach a wider age and interest range. We have integrated storytelling into these certificates:

- **Community Development and Engagement:** This 12-credit certificate is designed for people who want to become professional community organizers. Following the lead of Harvard's Marshall Ganz, storytelling is seen as a key tool for organizers at all levels. We offer the Art of Storytelling with a set of readings specifically designed to meet the needs and interests of organizers.

- **Entrepreneurial Studies:** We teach Using Storytelling in Business Settings as part of this 16-credit certificate offered by our Entrepreneurial Center, and we provide story coaching for students preparing for pitch contests. Students completing the 16-credit program of study are eligible to apply for a microfinance business loan from $500 to $2,500 with MariSol Federal Credit Union, and their story/pitch skills are very relevant for this.

- **Storytelling Skills for Business:** A cohort of 24 high school students in the college's Achieving a College Education Program are participating in Storytelling Skills for Business. Led by Marilyn Torres, this 43-credit program is the first pathway model to be offered at SMCC and is built around the story and communication skills necessary to be a successful entrepreneur. As the program entered its second year in the summer of 2016, students performed the first annual "Perfect Pitch" concert with the audience voting as potential investors. By the end of the second year, cohort students will be placed in local civic engagement internships. This will complement their international volunteerism as Youth Ambassadors for the Storytelling Institute's official charity "Bead for Life" and to apply their skills in service learning to women entrepreneurs in the country of Uganda in Central Africa. In the beginning of their third and final program year in the summer of 2017, students will be placed in internships within the career business sectors of their interest as part of integrating them into the college's Workforce Development initiative. Our cohort is expected to graduate as Junior ACE Scholars with their associate degrees in business in the spring of 2018 and transition to the university.

- **Storytelling Skills for Health-Care Professionals:** A new cohort pathway focusing on the movement to integrate the arts into the sciences (STEAM) is in the planning process. The use of storytelling skills for health-care professionals in the workforce was inspired by the Storytelling Institute's development of workshops for SMCC's Bilingual Nursing Program Mentorship Project funded by the Robert Wood Johnson Foundation to mentor incoming nurses into the profession to increase diversity in future leadership among nurses as caregivers in health care.

Community Interest

We offer a series of 1-credit courses specifically designed to apply to focused interests. The courses are Using Storytelling in Educational Settings, Business Settings, Advocacy Settings, Healing Settings, and Interpretive Settings. The most successful format for these classes has been two consecutive Saturdays.

Quality Programming

The Storytelling Institute has annually brought in nationally and internationally known tellers. It has been a great privilege to hear them perform and to learn from them in the workshops. I hope this continues!

—Storytelling Certificate Graduate, 2014

Providing our students, faculty, and the community with high-quality storytelling events with the best local and national storytellers is a cornerstone of the Storytelling Institute, and it serves several important purposes:

- It provides models for what good storytelling is and what it looks and feels like.
- It excites people, engages them, and creates interest in our classes and programs.
- It attracts community partners to help us extend our programming.
- It provides faculty, students, and the community with ongoing access to high-level training.

Our annual series and signature programs are rooted in traditional stories. We feel a responsibility to guard the flame of folktales, myths, and legends since so much of the storytelling in our country right now is based in personal experience. Myth-Informed in the fall and Folktales for Grown-Ups in the spring are meant to entertain and provide an opportunity for dialogue to deepen learning. These six concerts through the year allow us to explore myth and folktale in both serious and playful ways as we provide opportunities for our faculty, professionals from the community, and advanced students to develop programming.

One of the Myth-Informed nights, the riotously fun Greek and Roman Myth Throwdown has become an annual, and very well-attended, favorite in the community. Twenty-six tellers relate three-minute Greek and Roman myths from A to Z, and the audience votes for their seven favorites. Those seven then go on to perform in a follow-up concert, Classic Moves.

Myth-Mob, a performance group made up of full and adjunct faculty, put together several programs on themes for Myth-Informed that allowed us to mash-up popular culture and myth, including Three Goddesses and a Guy, You Don't Own Me, and Big Girls Who Fight. Other Myth-Informed nights have featured a single myth or mythic character like Gilgamesh, Osun—Goddess of the River, the story of Sogolon Condé—the mother of Sundiata, Brynhildr from the Völsunga saga, Cupid and Psyche, and the Story of the Grail. Each program is about an hour, with time afterward for dialogue with the teller or tellers.

Folktales for Grown-Ups, our spring series, usually features a specific tale type, culture area, or archetypal folktale character such as the trickster or the crone. These programs usually last about 90 minutes; always feature multiple tellers with a mix of faculty, students, and community tellers; last about an hour; and also allow time afterward for discussion on both the stories and storytelling.

Our signature program is Return to the African Village, produced every February in connection with African American History Month. Full-time faculty member Marilyn Torres was inspired by her deep personal connection to African oral traditions to create and produce this annual extravaganza of story, culture, drumming, and dance. Now entering our seventh year in 2017, Return to the African Village is built on the premise that a group of faculty and students have been touring Africa. They return to their host village to share their stories and are welcomed by the residents—the elders, storytellers, and children. Marilyn's vision is to create a sacred space through the production so that all present, on stage or in the audience, can experience the breadth, depth, and beauty of a living tradition.

During the two weeks leading up to the event, we hold our classes in Performance Hall as the stage is being built and decorated. Students received academic lectures and storytelling on the history of the movement of Africans during the "middle passage" that has resulted in a rich legacy of comingling of races and cultures from around the world. The week before the production, we bring in a featured teller to expand and deepen what is being learned. Connie Regan-Blake came in 2013 and introduced us to Bead for Life, which has become the institute's signature charity. Bobby Norfolk was our featured teller in 2014, and in 2015, we featured Lynette Ford, as we explored the connections between Native American and African traditions. In 2016, Antonio Rocha helped us celebrate the impact of Africa on Brazil. Every year we also feature a traditional dance and drumming group. For the first several years, this was a troupe based in African dance, Kawambe-Omowale Drum and Dance Theatre. This year we featured Axe Capoeira of Arizona, and between them, the storytellers and those serving as villagers, there were over 40 people on the stage.

To round out our calendar, we offer several other annual events:

- Donald Davis comes most years in the fall. In even-numbered years, he does a public concert and visits classes. In odd-numbered years, he does a weekend intensive.
- A Faculty Concert every January that includes stories from all the faculty and features one of the full-time or adjuncts, or a professional from the community.
- A Graduate Concert featuring stories from those who are completing their 30-credit storytelling certificate in that year.
- Tellabration on the Friday night before Thanksgiving.
- Student concerts as needed at the end of each semester.

Strong Internal and External Partnerships

On Feb. 14, 2011—one year to the day before the state's centennial— we launched Arizona Storytellers, a project designed to connect with readers wherever they turn. We couldn't have done it without the support and guidance of the amazing team at SMCC. Arizona Storytellers was and remains a collaborative community effort

*supported by South Mountain Community College and their certifi-
cate program in storytelling.*
   —Keira Nothaft, senior director, News Content and Product
      Development, the *Arizona Republic*, 2014

There is high demand for storytelling, both performance and training, from both our internal and external communities. In 2013, the full and adjunct faculty of the Storytelling Institute produced or participated in 62 events. Thirty-five of those events were internal to the college or district: The Storytelling Institute produced 21 events, and we participated or con-tributed to 14 other events with college or district partners. Those included the Achieving a College Education Program, the president's office, International/Intercultural Education, the South Mountain Community Library, the Gila River Indian Community Project, Student Life/ Leadership, Upward Bound, and Faculty Development.

Twenty-seven of the events in 2013 that we produced or participated in were for entities external to our college or district. Fourteen of those were for nonprofit entities, and thirteen were for corporate entities, the majority being with our major media outlet, the *Arizona Republic*.

Our two longest and deepest partnerships are with the Mesa Arts Center and the *Arizona Republic*. We began partnering with the Mesa Arts Center (MAC) in 2003 as part of the Mesa Storytelling Festival. We helped produce those events along with integrating a youth storytelling component. When the festival ended in 2009, we continued to partner with the MAC to bring in national-level storytellers. Partnering with the MAC allows us to leverage our resources. The national tellers we bring in can stay longer and reach more people as a result.

We have been in partnership with the *Arizona Republic* since 2010. Marilyn and I designed and facilitated a series of storytelling workshops to prepare people to video-record stories for the Arizona Storytellers' centennial website in the paper's yearlong lead-up to the state's centennial in February 2012. We also coproduced, coached, and emceed the Republic's tent at the two-day Centennial Celebration in 2012, which featured over 40 tellers and speakers.

Under the leadership of features reporter Megan Finnerty, the Republic began producing monthly nights of live storytelling in June 2012. We worked with Megan to design those nights and have provided committed, ongoing support by coaching tellers, recruiting tellers, and telling ourselves. Arizona Storytellers has caught fire in Phoenix, selling out in venues accommodating anything from 200 to 600 people. SMCC and the institute have been consis-tently included in the marketing and branding of these events in the paper and on the web. This has been a huge plus for the Storytelling Institute, has played a major role in increasing the public's knowledge of storytelling and the institute, and has also raised the profile of SMCC in the community.

Commitment to Diversity

*The faculty strives to build a community founded on respect, com-
munication, spirit and human warmth. The faculty is able to bring
a diverse range of community members together with the professional skill, time, and energy spent on instilling the institute's cultural values into their department, staff, and students.*
      —Storytelling Certificate Graduate, 2014

Reflecting the diversity of the student body and the community around the college is the foundation of the curriculum, staffing, and event programming in the Storytelling Institute. Creating a diverse, inclusive program has been the driving vision of our program since the beginning, and one that we have pursued with conscious diligence. Phoenix is bisected on its east-west axis by the Salt River. In the earlier part of the twentieth century, African Americans were forced to live south of Van Buren Street, and many settled in what was then the rural area below the river, which became known as South Phoenix, along with their Mexican American, Native American, and Japanese American neighbors. SMCC is located in South Phoenix, and it remains the part of town with the most ethnic and socioeconomic diversity. Responding to this heritage is not just a responsibility; it is a privilege, and one that has deepened and enriched the programming of the Storytelling Institute. A Eurocentric orientation would not only have failed our community, but it would also have failed our philosophy of storytelling and the role that storytelling has played around the world in human life and culture at the largest level.

We have pursued our commitment to diversity in three primary ways: through our coursework, programming, and faculty. Our required courses (the Art of Storytelling I and II, Multicultural Folktales I and II) by their nature include material from around the world as well as reflect the diversity of our nation. Our elective courses (Mythology, Telling Sacred Stories from around the World, African Storytelling Tradition, Irish Storytelling Tradition) are based in the world storytelling tradition or explore a particular culture in depth. Genre or context-based classes (Creating and Telling Personal Stories, Using Storytelling in a Variety of Settings) rely on the diversity that the participants themselves bring to the class. Similarly, our events are built to highlight diversity in both the content and the tellers, and our signature events like Return to the African Village and the new Elder Brother Native American festival specifically reflect the diversity of our community.

But diversity in our coursework and events would not mean much if our faculty was not diverse. From the beginning we have attracted and recruited a diverse faculty. Our current storytelling faculty includes members of African, Latin, Asian, Native, and European ancestry. They range in age from 30 to 60 plus and also include members of the LGBTQ community. This did not happen by accident. We specifically sought to create this diversity by recruiting, supporting, and encouraging likely candidates who came to our classes, our trainings, and our college and community events. We encourage them to take more storytelling classes, mentor them, integrate them into our training model, involve them in events, and eventually hire them in our classes at the college and around the district.

The Future of the Storytelling Institute

Storytelling has enabled me to recognize the commonalities that I have with others and appreciate the differences. Storytelling has allowed me to be open minded to ideas, philosophies, and quite possibly people that I might not have been had I not gone through the institute. I believe in the power of storytelling.
—Storytelling Certificate Graduate, 2014

The initial focus of our program was the folktales, myths, and legends of the world's oral storytelling traditions. The subsequent community need for, and interest in, personal, family, and fact-based stories has influenced our course content, our event programming, and our community outreach over time. We now have a college storytelling program that can offer the community a wide spectrum of storytelling skills training. Over the years, we have developed a reputation for the following:

- Well-trained, diverse faculty and continuous faculty and program improvement
- Innovative and high-quality course offerings
- Student success and opportunity
- Workforce relevance and application
- Multicultural respect and inclusivity
- Engaging and exciting college and community events
- Inclusive and collaborative internal partnerships
- High-impact external partnerships
- Commitment to service and integrity

We started with a vision of the power and relevance of a storytelling program at our community college, and that vision proved to be vividly true. Storytelling as an academic discipline, as an art form, and as a tool for building community has never been more relevant. Public interest in storytelling is at an all-time high. Now is the time to create storytelling programs in colleges and universities across our nation.

Enriching Minds, Encouraging Hope and Joy: Columbus Story Adventures—a Community-Outreach Program of the Storytellers of Central Ohio

Lyn Ford

As technology advances and the American economy becomes increasingly knowledge based, individuals must be able to read, write, and communicate at higher levels in order to succeed economically and socially.
—https://www.learnthat.org/pages/view/literacy_facts.html

In 2003, storyteller and teaching artist Sally Crandall experienced one of those "Aha!" brilliant moments of inspiration: our local storytelling group, Storytellers of Central Ohio, was (and is) a 501(c)(3) nonprofit-status organization, making it eligible for some grants, and also was expected to do charitable, educational, or literary activities of service for the community. Why not put together a project that offered literacy skills and storytelling to students in at-risk situations, in summer programs that might help them to maintain or improve their language-arts skill (reading, comprehension, speaking, and writing) levels for the next school year?

This bit of inspiration was based in Sally's knowledge as a former teacher and school librarian and a teaching artist with the Artists-in-Schools Program of the Greater Columbus Arts Council (this teaching-artist community programming is now under the umbrella of the Ohio Alliance for Arts Education). And, according to statistics listed from a 2007 study by D. R. Entwisle and L. L. Olson on their "Reading Is Fundamental" Literacy Facts & Stats page:

Summer is a critical time when students either leap ahead or fall behind.

- During the summer months, all children are at risk of losing some of the learning obtained during the school year.
- This is especially true for children from low-income families.
- More than 80 percent of children from economically disadvantaged communities lose reading skills over the summer because they lack access to books, learning resources, and such enrichment opportunities as trips to the library, bookstore, or museum.
- Students who lose reading ability over the summer rarely catch up.
- Over time, the summer learning slide can add up to the equivalent of three years of reading loss by the end of fifth grade.

Sally's idea was of value to the Columbus area and to the Storytellers of Central Ohio. She shared her idea with two of her friends and fellow storytellers, Beverly Comer and Lynette Ford. And all three got that "yes!" feeling. In agreement, they laughed and said, "Let's do it!"

Then reality kicked in. Although Storytellers of Central Ohio had its nonprofit status and a solid core group of storytellers who were experienced working with children of all ages, it had no grant writers in place, no huge funders for events, and very little money. That meant that Crandall, Comer, and Ford would become the initiators of a new project; the authors of the statement of purpose and plan of operations for that project; the program promoters giving sales pitches to potential partners; the first volunteer storytellers for the project; and the crazed and sometimes frustrated money seekers for a project that did not even have a name.

The three gave it a name: Columbus Story Adventures (CSA). The initial project concept included:

- stories shared in the oral tradition, told by diverse storytellers, so that the young people could hear a diversity of language usage and various styles of narrative communication;
- corresponding connections to stories in literary format that were appropriate for the various grade levels for which we might work;
- workshop activities created by each teller, in a format that included the needs of all types of learners (or as many types of learners as we could discern in contact with our partnering organizations) to encourage and enrich literacy skills; and
- free books for all participating students.

It was determined that the project would have to run for at least six weeks in order to have any kind of impact on the reading, speaking, and writing skills of participating students. We also determined that central Ohio had many neighborhood organizations where such a project would be worthwhile as a part of the offerings of summer programs.

The concept went from ideas on paper to active program in 2004. And, with Sally Crandall still in a leadership position, Beverly Comer and Lyn Ford still active on the committee, and solid support from bighearted storytelling volunteers (who only receive gas money for their trips to and from the various sites where they perform, and who often refuse to accept even that), the CSA project has continued, and increased its partnerships in the community, for twelve years.

Crandall, Comer, and Ford first set up a practical and very simple budget—what we would need to get things started. Would we pay for storyteller's work or expect all participating storytellers to volunteer their services? Where would we offer this program? And, where would we find the money needed to begin? Having decided that any monetary compensation a storyteller received would be dependent upon what funds could be raised and on what the project needed to support it (the first costs considered books; promotional flyers; and an enrichment guide for educators and mentors), the three sought appropriate funding possibilities and began the process of applying for grants.

The first grant application (accepted and received!) was from the Paul G. Duke Foundation, whose focus was programs benefiting children, young adults, and families, and which no longer accepts grant applications for the central Ohio community (Crandall, Comer, and Ford learned to be aware of what's available, what's expected in the application, and how things change over time—they do change!). The grant helped get the ball rolling and lasted for one year. By that time, CSA members had learned that it was much easier for partnering organizations to apply for and receive literacy grants that included the CSA project in their planning than it was for CSA to qualify for such grants on its own. But other grants, funds, and donations of books came over the past twelve years from St. John's Episcopal Church, Target, Thrivent Financial for

Lutherans (a financial planning and wealth-management organization), Borders Bookstores, Books for Kids to Keep, and First Book Columbus.

In the past, CSA also held fund-raisers called "Story Soup"; these were soup-and-bread luncheons that included a silent auction and a story concert, supported by the volunteerism of our organization. Various soups were made by members of the Storytellers of Central Ohio, whether or not they were active members of the CSA committee, and a variety of fresh breads was donated by Panera as well as by the membership of SOCO and CSA; beverages and cookies were also donated. All proceeds went to CSA's budget. This fund-raiser was held for three years, and then it was no longer needed, thanks to the generosity of supporting grants and donations. A sample invitation is included at the end of this article.

Many of CSA's books were donated by First Book, a nonprofit organization dedicated to overcoming illiteracy; according to the information available on its website, "First Book is transforming the lives of children in need and elevating the quality of education by making new, high-quality books available on an ongoing basis." Books have also been donated in the past by individuals and by used-book stores such as Half Price Books, leading the committee to go through the many boxes of donations and find those books that were in like-new condition and of interest to the grade levels with whom we might work—a big task that took a lot of time and effort, but we were grateful for the assistance in our early years.

With a larger budget now available to CSA, the committee annually takes advantage of the Scholastic Book warehouse sales, "exclusively for librarians, teachers, school employees and volunteers, Book Fair chairpeople, and homeschool teachers"; because CSA works within the criteria expected (volunteers in school settings), committee members attend these events as a team, fanning out and finding the books needed at prices 50–80 percent off selected clearance items. CSA also has high-quality books in storage from past years, reducing the number of books needed to initiate the summer book giveaways.

CSA still accepts donations for this program. Records of its activities are kept in accordance with regulations for the Storytellers of Central Ohio 501(c)(3) nonprofit-status designation.

CSA is now a very active community-outreach committee of the Storytellers of Central Ohio, in which approximately 12–15 storytellers actively participate as both planners and presenters in any year. The committee is open to any dues-paying members of Storytellers of Central Ohio; but to become involved as a performing member of the committee, one must be*:

- a teaching artist with the Greater Columbus Arts Council, Ohio Arts Council, Thurber House's writing programs for young people, or one of the community arts organizations of the Ohio Alliance for Arts Education;

- an experienced teller who has effectively worked in schools for more than two years;

- a former educator or media specialist who has worked with children at some grade level between pre-K through 12; or

- someone whom CSA committee members have observed several times as he or she worked with children so that some members can attest to the teller's ability to effectively offer performances and workshops to the CSA programming.

CSA's approach to encouraging, nurturing, and reinforcing a love of reading and effectively communicating, writing, and listening to stories is a six-week project that includes storytelling, literacy workshops, and the gift of six books for every child in the program. This programming is offered to summer camps, schools, and various child-supporting and family-supporting centers throughout central Ohio. Events are held on-site in classrooms, gymnasiums, outdoor settings (when the weather permits), and multi-purpose rooms, wherever there is available, accessible space for the teller, children, and mentors. CSA's storytellers strive to encourage and strengthen reading, speaking, and writing skills for children in "at-risk" situations—homelessness, life in unsafe and unsupportive neighborhoods, and circumstances in which academic enrichment is low and grade-level language-arts skills might decrease during the summer months.

CSA provides the staff of each organization with an informative workshop and an idea-filled handbook to use before and after CSA visits (a sample page from this handbook is included at the end of this article). Once a week for six weeks a storyteller visits; that teller spends 45 minutes telling stories to the children, eye to eye and heart to heart. Storytelling sessions are followed up with 30–60-minute workshops (dependent upon the venue's scheduling and the age/skill levels of the students). The workshops allow the children to respond to the stories by writing or telling their own stories, responding to the stories they have heard through visual art or movement, creating poetry or parallel stories, and singing corresponding songs and interactive story play—whatever will enhance the story session and make it memorable and increase the probability of comprehension and retention of the language skills modeled and utilized.

CSA also provides a free book for every child after every visit, giving each child a small library of six books. This is sometimes a very emotional experience for both the tellers and the students as well as the teachers. Tellers have witnessed tears and comments such as "I never owned a book before!" or sheer disbelief—"This is mine? I get to keep this book? I don't have to give it back?"; tellers have also seen children hug their books as if they were stuffed animals and delight in writing their names in the front covers of their very own books.

Although the programs are generally planned for six weeks during the summer, CSA's activities have sometimes been requested during the school year, too. And we do them. Members have carried this project to:

- Columbus's South Side Settlement House (which closed its doors in 2011 after 112 years of service to some of the city's poorest people);

- The Dowd Center, an academically focused after-school and summer program, which follows the curriculum of the Columbus City Schools under the auspices of the Homeless Families Foundation;

- Gladden House, a settlement house "providing education and recreation programs, emergency assistance, and advocacy and support for individuals, families, and groups";

- The Hispanic Coalition, whose mission is "to improve the well-being and quality of life for all Hispanics/Latinos through advocacy, education, training, and access to quality services";

- Rachel Muha's Run the Race Program, which "gathers children together for free after-school and Saturday programs";

- St. John Learning Center, which offers free General Education Degree (GED) classes and computer training for out-of-school youth and adults; and
- St. Stephens Community House's daycare center; St. Stephens provides community services, including emergency food assistance, job readiness workshops, the daycare center, and refugee services.

It is difficult to be sure of the number of students with whom CSA members have worked. Populations at these sites are often in transition, and the numbers in attendance at CSA events greatly fluctuate at times. But it is estimated that CSA has touched the lives and minds of approximately 180 students each summer, totaling more than 2,000 students in grades pre-K through 12 over the past twelve years. That also means CSA has given approximately 12,000 books away!

Members of CSA now realize that the little "Aha!" moment Sally had years ago has led to something that offers much more than literacy enrichment and storytelling. The program offers hope and joy to many children who have never heard a story *told* and never owned a book. It also offers a model of personal creativity and achievement to older students, who have said things like "I never knew you could be a storyteller. I could do that! Where do I find more stories?"

Participation in each of the arts as creators, performers, and audience members enables individuals to discover and develop their own creative capacity, thereby providing a source of lifelong satisfaction...Participation in the arts as creators, performers, and audience members (responders) enhances mental, physical, and emotional wellbeing.
　　　　　—From the Philosophical Foundations of the National Core Arts Standards, http://www.nationalartsstandards.org/content/conceptual-framework

For more information about CSA, contact:
Jim Flanagan at jirish@ohiohills.com
Sally Crandall at scrandall@earthlink.net

*Note:** These days, working with young people in the state of Ohio requires background checks. Teaching artists must have these done as a requirement of their continued work in schools and other education venues. Usually, members who want to share with young people already have a background check on file with some arts/education/service organization, or they can easily get one started by going to Action for Children (http://www.actionforchildren.org/), a resource and referral agency for child care and early learning services in central Ohio. The cost is minimal. The background check is absolutely necessary.

Bibliography

Alexander, K. L. "Lasting Consequences of the Summer Learning Gap." *American Sociological Review* 72, no. 4 (2007): 167–180.
FirstBook, https://www.firstbook.org/.
"The Literacy Crisis." Reading Is Fundamental. http://www.rif.org/about-rif/literacy-crisis/.

Sample Invitation for CSA's "Story Soup" Fund-raiser

STORY SOUP!

A SIMPLE LUNCH OF HEARTY SOUPS, BREADS & DESSERTS, SILENT AUCTION, & STORYTELLING PERFORMANCE

Proceeds benefit Columbus Story Adventures, SOCO's literacy outreach program

About Columbus Story Adventures—Storytellers of Central Ohio (SOCO) have implemented a literacy outreach program called Columbus Story Adventures (CSA). We provide each partnering organization with an informative staff workshop and an idea-filled handbook to use before and after CSA visits. Once a week, for six weeks, a storyteller visits the site, spending 45 minutes telling stories to the children—it's done eye-to-eye and heart-to-heart. After each session the teller provides an enrichment time—where the children can respond to, write about, or retell the stories—along with other fun literacy activities. After each visit, CSA provides a free book for every child to keep.

CSA has partnered with (list partners here)

WE HOPE YOU CAN JOIN US!

*****Cut here and send this information*****

Columbus Story Adventures STORY SOUP! RSVP by _____

1 person—$20 (donation for attendance is tax deductible) # of people _____

Couple—$35 (donation for attendance is tax deductible)

Make check payable to Storytellers of Central Ohio

Name(s) (Please Print) _____

Address: _____

Email: _____ Phone Number: _____

I'm unable to attend. Please accept my donation of $_____

Mail to:

If you have a product or service you would like to donate to the silent auction, we would appreciate your contribution! Please contact (   ) at (   )

We are happy to announce that Thrivent Financial for Lutherans will match $1 for every $3 we make, up to $1000!

Storytellers of Central Ohio is a non-profit, 501c(3) organization—www.socotales.org

Sample CSA Activity, Grade Level K–2

(from a portion of a CSA event facilitated by Lyn Ford)

A Trip to the Moon

Stories told: "Skunk Loved the Moon," a Native American folktale (specific culture unknown)

"Anansi the Spider: How the Moon Came to Be in the Sky," a folktale from Ghana

Story activity:

1. Participants will discuss what they "know" about the moon, what they think they know about the moon, and what they might see or can imagine about the moon. The storyteller will take notes on all statements made.

2. Participants will take an imaginary, interactive trip to the moon in a rocket or on the space shuttle; the trip will be accompanied by the music of Bobby McFerrin, *Bang! Zoom!* The storyteller will encourage participants to put on space suits, prepare themselves for the journey, feel the take-off, exit their space ship and move around on the moon and observe what they can throughout their unique adventures on the moon and the trip back home (or wherever each individual decides to be).

3. After the trip, participants will put their space suits away, and tell their individual stories in response to the opening phrase, "I took a trip to the moon, and I saw..." Storyteller will facilitate and guide the narration from its beginning through its middle highlight to its end: "I came back home" or "I went to Mars" or "I stayed on the moon," etc.

4. Participants will draw the highlight of their moon adventure on a white paper plate (round like the moon) with crayons.

Book connections

- Dayrell, Elphinstone. *Why the Sun and the Moon Live in the Sky*. Logan, Iowa: Perfection Learning, 2010. ISBN-10: 0812485645; ISBN-13: 978-0812485646.
- Brown, Margaret Wise. *Goodnight Moon*. New York: HarperCollins, 2007. ISBN-10: 0060775858; ISBN-13: 978-0060775858.

Taking the Stage: The Lone Star Student Storyteller Program

Bonnie Barber, Cindy Boatfield, Lisa Bubert,
Julie Chappell, Jennifer Cummings, and Mayra Diaz

The History of the Lone Star Storytelling Festival Student Storyteller Program

The Lone Star Storytelling Festival, originally named the Frisco Storytelling Festival, was launched in 2004 by the Frisco Public Library Foundation. The goal of the Festival was, and remains, to serve as a fundraiser to support the Library endowment fund and ensure the financial health of the Frisco Public Library. Inspired by the Timpanogos Storytelling Festival in Orem, Utah, Shelley Holley (Frisco Public Library director), the Foundation board, and support staff agreed that an annual storytelling festival would be a fitting way to raise funds and support for the Frisco Public Library and provide a unique cultural and literary event for the community.

Based on the large youth population in the Frisco area, a community that delights in supporting youth achievement, the Student Storyteller Program was created to complement the Festival. Children ages 8–18 audition to become a student storyteller, are mentored by storytelling professionals, and perform alongside the professional artists. Auditions filled up quickly the first year, and the Student Storyteller Program was born!

Community Collaboration and Funding of the Lone Star Storytelling Festival

The Foundation members found success in their fund-raising efforts, receiving grants, corporate funds, and thousands of dollars of in-kind donations for performer lodging, catering, and event publicity in exchange for a valuable spot on the Festival's sponsor list. In addition, volunteers lined up to contribute hundreds of work hours to the event's success.

Shelley Holley and support staff recognized that while the event served as great family entertainment, it also held strong educational value in regard to the history of oral tradition. In early planning stages, Holley reached out to the Frisco Independent School District (FISD) administrators, inviting entire grade levels to attend the proposed storytelling festival as a field/study trip. The administrators recognized the benefit to students, and a new partnership was forged that continues to this day. Attending the Festival's "Field Trip Day" is now a highly anticipated tradition among FISD fourth-grade classes. Leading up to the Festival, students discuss the importance of storytelling in different cultures, read and share various folktales, and practice audience etiquette. Of course, much of the student excitement for Field Trip Day is due in part to the featured student storytellers who are often their fellow classmates.

Program Scope

Students interested in becoming student storytellers must submit an application and audition video. The application includes an Agreement

Form that must be signed by a parent or guardian that includes permission to release photos and interviews to the press. Students may audition as individuals or in pairs. Storytellers are selected by a panel of judges.

Once chosen, student storytellers attend a mandatory orientation meeting and coaching sessions to learn storytelling techniques and practice their performances. Students receive feedback from coaches and their peers.

Prior to the Festival, students practice their performances at community concerts and a dress rehearsal. During the Festival, student storytellers share the stage with nationally known professional storytellers. Student storytellers are not compensated, but they do receive complimentary Festival tickets. Throughout the year, student storytellers may be asked to perform at other events. The benefits of being a student storyteller include building public speaking skills, building confidence, and developing an appreciation of other cultures through the oral tradition of storytelling.

Audience

The Student Storyteller Program is open to students ages 8–18. Students are typically Frisco residents, though participants may come from other school districts or attend home school. Festival audiences include all ages from the Frisco area.

How-To Guide

School Partnership

The Student Storyteller Program would not be successful without a strong partnership with the FISD. Each spring, Library staff attend elementary and secondary school librarian meetings to promote the program and distribute posters. School librarians encourage students to audition, and many offer assistance with audition videos. One school had their student storyteller perform at a school assembly. This was a wonderful opportunity for that storyteller, and it was very well received by her fellow students.

Our two Field Trip Day concerts give some of our finest student storytellers the opportunity to perform along with the professional storytellers and tell their stories to an audience of approximately 2,500 fourth-grade FISD students and teachers. Student storytellers consider it an honor to perform at Field Trip Day concerts and come away feeling like a rock star!

Publicity

The Library uses a variety of outlets to promote the Student Storyteller Program so that students, parents, teachers, and school librarians are informed of the Festival and the audition process. Many promotional efforts are digital, such as a web banner on the Library website featuring photos of previous Student Storytellers in action, along with a link to audition details. A slide promoting auditions is uploaded to flat-screen monitors in the Library/City Hall atrium, and information is also posted on the Library's social media platforms.

In addition, we display posters and application forms in the Library. Audition information is featured on the Library's spring class schedule. Press releases are also sent out to local newspapers and online media outlets, and auditions are advertised at local theaters and after-school groups. All

Student Storyteller (Marianna) performs at the Dr. Pepper Arena on Field Trip Day.

promotional materials direct students and parents to www.lonestarstories. org, our dedicated Festival website. There we house the most current, detailed information regarding all aspects of the Festival and the Student Storyteller Program. We also provide resources for auditionees, such as tips and video examples of successful auditions, benefits of being a Student Storyteller, expectations of selected Student Storytellers, audition FAQs, and other valuable storytelling information.

Auditions and Judging

The Library opens auditions for a two-month period and requires students be 8–18 years old. We accept auditions via DVD or YouTube video. (Tip: Students should e-mail YouTube links since handwritten URLs on the application form are tricky to decipher.)

Library staff gather a panel to judge audition videos. Judges may be Library staff, volunteers, local storytellers, or drama teachers. We recommend including everyone who will be a student storyteller coach. Depending on submissions, judging may take two or more weeks to complete. Our judging system awards points for the elements deemed important (see sample Judging Form). After all submissions have been judged, we tally and average points. We decide the number of students we can

Student Storyteller audition clickable web banner featuring past Student Storytellers.

successfully handle in the program and take that number of top scores, usually 8–11 students.

All students who audition are contacted with results by e-mail. Staff encourage those not selected to audition again next year and offers tips for future success. For students who are selected, we extend congratulations and provide information about orientation (see sample Orientation Documents).

Orientation

We like to have a Library manager or director attend orientation to welcome students and parents to the program and to congratulate them on being selected. We also review program details:

Points to cover include the following (see sample Orientation Documents):

- Introductions (coaches and students)
- Communication (methods, expectations)
- Coaching sessions (number required, sign up, expectations)
- Community concerts (number required, sign up, expectations)
- Dress rehearsal concert (date, place)

- Agreement Form (review program expectations and collect signed forms)
- Student Biographical Form (fill out and collect)
- Publicity photos (take individual head shots)
- Story choice (if needed, new stories are selected from provided books or stories)
- Questions from students and parents

Coaching Sessions

Student storytellers must attend coaching sessions in order to feel confident on stage and perform well when concert day arrives. Running a strong coaching session, where the storytellers feel encouraged, supported, and safe, is essential to growing confident performers. The quality of the coaching sessions can make or break the performance experience for the student.

We require student storytellers to successfully complete seven coaching sessions before they are deemed fully "stage ready," though they may be asked to attend more if the coaches feel it is needed. We offer, on average, three coaching sessions a week at five or seven in the evening to accommodate student schedules. Students and parents can select coaching sessions online through www.signupgenius.com so they can reserve their spot and the coaches know who to expect at each practice. Coaching sessions, usually run by one staff coach and a volunteer if available, are limited to five students per hour to ensure everyone gets enough time to practice. Parents are not permitted to watch these practice sessions.

Parents are not allowed to attend coaching sessions for many reasons. First and foremost, we strive to create an environment of trust where any student feels free to experiment and make mistakes as part of the learning process. It is also imperative that constructive criticism comes only from trained coaching staff who are experts in stage performance and know how to deliver suggestions to young artists without damaging their confidence or trust. Involved parents are encouraged to read the written coaching session notes we give each student, celebrate the praise given, and help their student practice the recommended improvements at home.

Coaches lead a group warm-up activity, and then each storyteller performs his or her story, either in its entirety or in selected pieces. Coaches time the telling to ensure students are falling within the performance time limit. The coach also notes praise and critique received during the session. Praises, or appreciations, are given by both coaches and students. Critiques, however, may come only from the coaching team. All comments are documented in a coaching folder, and copies are sent home with each student so they remember what worked well and what they have for "homework."

A good coach must have the ability to critique the young performer in a way that encourages his or her creative growth. Receiving applause and appreciation from fellow students builds a sense of community within the group, increases trust during practice, and provides confidence on stage.

Concerts

Prior to the Festival, we schedule several small concerts to give student storytellers practice in front of an audience at venues such as library events, local bookstores, senior centers, the Boys and Girls Club, and Toastmaster meetings. These take place toward the end of the coaching cycle, just prior

Student Storytellers at dress rehearsal.

to the Festival. We use www.signupgenius.com, a collaborative scheduling tool, to allow students/parents to sign up for concerts (as well as coaching sessions) that fit their schedule. Family and friends are encouraged to attend concerts. The Student Storyteller lineup for community and Festival concerts is carefully planned, taking into account story length, topic, and presentation style. Strongest performers go in anchor spots (first and last) to set everyone up for success. A coach or other Library staff serves as the emcee for concerts. The coach arrives early, greets students, provides the order of performers, and provides instructions for stage or microphone matters. The coach introduces each storyteller and distributes promotional materials for the Festival if appropriate. We also make sure to thank each venue for hosting a concert.

The dress rehearsal is a mandatory concert that provides students their final practice before the big day. It is a good time to confirm the Festival schedule and distribute final materials, such as:

- schedules and maps for all events;
- access badges (for students and parents);
- complimentary tickets to events; and
- certificates of appreciation for students (signed by the Library director and president of the Library Foundation).

We congratulate and thank participants for their hard work and commitment and take lots of pictures—especially a group picture of the storytellers with their certificates!

Student Storyteller (Teresa) performs in Council Chambers during the Festival.

Student Storytellers who did not perform at Field Trip Day get to share the stage with professional storytellers during the Lone Star Storytelling Festival in a series of concerts. Four public concerts, which run Friday night through Saturday night of the Festival, feature two Student Storytellers interspersed among the professionals. After each concert, the Student Storytellers sign autographs and chat with audience members alongside the pros. Student Storytellers are also invited to attend one of several master classes presented by the professional storytellers; we waive the class fee for these students whenever possible. Over the course of the Festival weekend, every Student Storyteller has a chance to shine, learn from peers and professionals, and enjoy the spoils of their hard work.

After the Festival

After the Festival, we send a "congratulations and thank you" e-mail to parents and Student Storytellers. We include rave reviews and an invitation to audition again next year. We also send a survey to students, volunteers, and staff. Evaluation of the Student Storyteller Program is done annually with the help of the coaching team, and we document changes for the following year.

Student Storyteller (Caleb) performs in Council Chambers during the Festival.

Conclusion

This information reflects the current model of the Lone Star Student Storyteller Program at the Frisco Public Library. Through our 12 years, the program has seen many changes and will continue to evolve, as we are always looking for ways to streamline and improve our efforts. Our Library staff agree that being a Student Storyteller coach is one of the most rewarding job duties we have in our Youth Services Division. We hope you will find the same is true for you and your Library staff!

2015 Lone Star Student Storyteller Audition Application

- Application and Audition Deadline: Sunday, May 3, 2015 at 6 pm. Please turn in to the Frisco Public Library, 2nd Floor Ask Us! Desk or 1st floor Teen Room. Application and YouTube links can be emailed to:
- Audition DVDs will become property of the Frisco Public Library and will not be returned.

--------Cut here and enclose the completed form below with your audition video ---------

Lone Star Storytelling Festival 2015 Student Storyteller Audition Form

Student Name_____

Title of story (Please make sure to write your name and the title of your story on the DVD.)
_____

Please specify audition format (Circle One.)
DVD   **PC Compatible CD**   **YouTube URL**

Student:
_____
Age   Grade   Name of School   School Address

Parent or Guardian Name
_____

Student Home Address
_____
Street Address   City   State   Zip

Student Phone Number (Please indicate Cell or Home) _____

Parent's Cell or Work Phone Number (Please indicate Cell or Home) _____

Parent or Guardian's E-mail Address _____

For more information Contact:
Frisco Public Library, 6101 Frisco Square Blvd, Suite 3000, Frisco, Texas 75034
972.292.5669 ● 972.292.5699 (fax) ● Email:
Or visit lonestarstories.org

Sample Audition Application

Anecdotes/Quotes

The following quotes are from parents regarding their child's participation in the Student Storyteller Program:

> *Teresa thinks the Student Teller program is lots of fun, has helped her work on her speaking skills and gives her the added bonus of getting to meet other kids like her.*
>
> *I watched my daughter tell her story when she auditioned for the Storytelling Festival and again at the concerts and was amazed at how her story had come to life. Thank you so much for the coaching sessions!*
>
> *Our three children loved gaining confidence and developing their talents by performing with their peers and professional storytellers.*
>
> *It has been amazing to see how much our daughter has grown in the three years she has participated. It is not in the storytelling skills only, she has been provided with tools she can use for life.*

Bibliography

Lipman, Doug. *The Storytelling Coach: How to Listen, Praise, and Bring out People's Best*. Little Rock, AR: August House, 1995.

Watts, Nannette. *Youth Tell: Starting a Youth Storytelling Festival*. Highland, UT: Swift Publishing, 2004.

Sample Orientation Documents

Frisco Public Library Foundation
2015 Lone Star Storytelling Festival
Lone Star Student Storyteller Agreement Form

We understand and agree to the following:

- **A student storyteller is required to attend:**
  - Orientation
  - A minimum of 7 coaching sessions
  - One Special Performance/Community Concert
  - Student Storyteller Dress Rehearsal
  - FISD Field Trip Day, Thursday, October 15th or Friday, October 16th or the Lone Star Storytelling Festival on Saturday October 17, 2015.

- **Story Selection**
  - The story must be approved by coaching staff.
  - The story must be under 7 minutes in length.
  - Content of the story should be suitable for a family friendly audience, not contain any physical force to injure or abuse, any aggressive name calling or any bullying unless approved by coaches.

- **Coaching Sessions**
  - Coaching sessions are held in the 2nd floor Children's Program Room.
  - Coaching sessions last 1 hour.
  - Students must stay for the full session time to receive credit toward the 7 required sessions.
  - When a student is 10 minutes late that session will not count toward the required 7 sessions.
  - No more than 5 students during each coaching session.
  - There are no private coaching sessions unless requested by a coach.

- **Stage Readiness**
  - Should a student require additional assistance a coach will schedule private coaching sessions.
  - Should festival time arrive and a student is not ready to perform, the coaches reserve the right to excuse the student from their obligation to perform during the Lone Star Storytelling Festival.
  - Storytelling is an art meant to focus on the story and the teller. Theatrical elements (props, costuming, etc.) are not recommended. If a student feels strongly that such an item would enhance his or her performance it must be pre-approved by coaches during the coaching session process.

- **Compensation**
  - No student will receive compensation for performances other than (4) tickets for Saturday daytime and (4) tickets for the Friday Evening Concert **or** Saturday Evening Concert.

- **Media (parents or legal guardian)**
  - Pictures, recordings, and interviews of my student storyteller may be used in newspapers, brochures, flyers, the Lone Star Storytelling website or other social media.

Name of Student Storyteller (please print)

_____

Student Signature _____ **Date** _____

Name of parent or legal guardian (please print):

_____

Signature: _____ **Date** _____

Orientation, Coaching Sessions and Special Performances

Mandatory Orientation Session

Tuesday, July 28

7:15 pm–8:00 pm

2nd Floor Children's Program Room

Required for all Student Storytellers

Please bring your signed agreement form and completed biography. We will take pictures so dress for a "head shot." Stories will be available for students to browse if it was recommended he or she choose a new one.

Coaching Sessions

We offer scheduling options on SignUpGenius.com. You will receive an email invitation to SignUpGenius.com. Many session dates and times will be available so that your student may easily attend the required 7 sessions.

Community Concerts

Each teller is required to participate in **one** Special Performance of their choice. You will sign up using SignUpGenius. Please arrive 15 minutes prior to concert time and check in with your coach. Family and friends are welcome unless otherwise specified.

Dress Rehearsal

Sunday, October 11, 2015

3–5pm

Black Box Theatre—Frisco Arts/Sci-Tech Discovery Center

Family and friends encouraged to attend.

Required for all Student Storytellers

Lone Star Storytelling Festival

Field Trip Days: Thursday and Friday October 15 & 16 at Dr. Pepper Arena (invitation only)

Festival: Saturday, October 17 at the Frisco Public Library

Students will receive their schedule with details via e-mail approximately 2 weeks prior to the festival. No more than 4 students will be selected to tell on Field Trip days. Students who perform on Field Trip days will not perform at Saturday's Festival, but are encouraged to attend.

2015 Lone Star Storytelling Festival

Lone Star Student Storyteller

Biographical Information

Please keep in mind that your responses may be used by the emcee to share with an audience or with news reporters. Your answers will help the audience get to know you a little better.

Name _____ Age as of October 15th, 2015 _____

Grade you are entering this fall _____ School _____

By what name would you like the emcee to introduce you?

_____

Five adjectives that describe you.

_____

One thing few people know about you. (Example: you knit in your spare time)

_____

_____

The funniest thing that ever happened to you and/or your family?

_____

_____

Your most embarrassing moment. (Remember, we could use this to introduce you)

_____

_____

The best piece of advice or wisdom your mom or dad ever gave you.

_____

_____

What is your fondest memory?

_____

_____

Why did you audition to be a student storyteller?

_____

_____

The National Youth Storytelling Showcase

Nannette Watts

Mission

Strengthening storytelling by promoting and teaching the art of story among young tellers.

Vision

To empower the nation's youth through storytelling.

Madi sat on the floor of her classroom with sweaty palms. All of the third-grade classes were piled into one room. She let out a slow inaudible sigh—*Maybe they won't have time. Maybe I won't have to tell.* Her fear bound her so much that she hardly heard the other students tell. Then one boy told a story of a giant troll and a little boy outsmarting him. She laughed in spite of herself, right out loud, and she was taken away in the story. Madi was clapping wildly with the other students as he sat down pleased. Suddenly Mr. Crandall called, "Madi, it's your turn. Will you tell?"

Mr. Crandall was a caring and kind teacher. If she could not tell for herself, surely she could do it for Mr. Crandall. He believed in her. He said she could do it. Even with so much going on outside of school, the dark circles under her eyes proving she had little sleep, she could tell the other children and teachers her story; but there were so many of them.

Mr. Crandall walked over to the girl. He whispered something to her that she and fellow classmates heard. The children sitting next to her whispered, "Come on Madi, you can do it. Please tell us your story."

Madi was determined. She had a story to tell, and this was her chance to show the whole third grade she could do it. Her mind willed her body to unbind itself and stand. She rose from her place, slow but moving, until she was standing in the storytelling space at the front of the room.

She breathed in deeply and as she exhaled, the whole room exhaled with her. "Once there was a great ogre..." As Madi got to the end of the first phrase, some children laughed. Madi knew some of the children were enjoying her story, so she continued. More children and even some teachers and parents laughed too. Madi relaxed and shared the pictures she saw moving in the story in her head, and she knew everyone in the class could "see it" too.

When Madi finished her story, everyone in the room erupted with applause and shouts of "Great job Madi! You did it!" Mr. Crandall gave Madi a big thumbs-up and one of his warm smiles. "You did it! I knew you could."

Madi did not win the third-grade storytelling competition that day, but she did not care. She had accomplished something much more important.

These stories happen every year in classrooms across the United States —success stories for one child and for whole classrooms, as they learn the power story plays in their lives. There are successes both small and large for individuals at school, home, or community centers. Some excel in the art of telling stories, while others are happy to conquer the fear of standing in front of their peers telling a story; all are learning valuable leadership skills without really realizing it.

Some classrooms feed into a school storytelling festival by selecting their top teller or two and even moving on to share their stories at a school assembly. Other programs are held among homeschoolers who practice and gather to share stories together. Libraries offer programs where youth can see stories told well.

Young tellers or their family members may need to create the chance to tell stories. They can then participate in storytelling in local and regional opportunities.

The benefits of stories told are felt by both the teller who tells and the audience who also experience the stories. Stories impact the brain by teaching story structure and problem solving. Youth profit from their experiences with storytelling through increased test scores, being more motivated, and learning at a deeper level.

Young people all over the United States are telling stories each year. Some youth are telling stories in clubs or with their libraries or communities. Storytelling is an age-old art that is making a comeback but is not known or understood in some areas. Many times the young people telling stories in their schools and communities do not realize there are others, just like them, who are also telling stories in other parts of the United States.

Imagine the power of young people learning there are others just like them who participate in this great art of storytelling. They could learn they are not alone, that they are connected through a unique talent with other youth across the nation. If they could come together to tell stories and hear each other tell, they could become unified through this great art form. One lady imagined this very thing. In the late 1980s, Dr. Flora Joy tried to gather young people with this very idea in mind.

For nine years, she tried to get a youth storytelling program going, but participants were scarce. The original intent for the National Youth Storytelling event was to increase youth storytelling throughout the nation. Joy said, "The sole purpose of this event is to promote and encourage both the art and science of storytelling among pre-adult communicators."

Competition was not part of the original vision. It was a celebration of storytelling for youth. It was to instruct and encourage young tellers in the art. For a time, Flora found that a competition brought more participants. So, she added a competition in order to accomplish sharing the benefits of storytelling. She founded the National Storytelling Youth Olympics in 1996 to celebrate the accomplishments of young storytellers.

For six years, East Tennessee State University sponsored the program under the direction of Professor Flora Joy. In 2002, the program moved to a new location in central California with Executive Director Kevin Cordi and remained there for three years. Pigeon Forge, Tennessee, became hosts in 2005 with Elizabeth Rose holding the reins. The name changed in 2005 from the National Storytelling Youth Olympics to the National Youth Storytelling Hall of Fame and then the National Youth Storytelling Showcase (NYSS) in 2006. In 2011, a new home was needed, and the NYSS moved to Utah to be part of Timpanogos Storytelling, with Nannette Watts as director.

After many years of building a successful program, the time came to return to Flora Joy's original intent. The part families enjoyed most about participating in the National Youth Storytelling events was actually the source of what she had hoped to share: a love of storytelling, building the future of storytelling, and connecting with other youth storytellers from other parts of the nation. The part families did not enjoy was focusing on the competition instead of enjoying time with other storytellers and their families. As a competition is an end and stopping point, it negated the goal of this event.

The goal of the NYSS is to encourage every classroom in America to discover (or rediscover) the beauty and value of storytelling and story performance.

—Dr. Flora Joy

In a day when our focus has turned to rigorous testing for results—a day when young people know how to stare at a screen but do not know how to look a person in the eyes—researchers are proving the value and power of stories to teach in concise, precise, and exact ways. Reaching as many youth as possible across our nation through stories should continue to be our goal. As our nation awakens to the reality that removing the arts from schools has not helped students improve, we can begin to learn the great power of story to teach and motivate.

The NYSS is actually the end and the beginning. There is competition leading up to this final event. Thousands of youth tell stories in classroom, home, community, and state competitions and can be selected to represent their state at an even larger gathering. Storytellers can be ages 8–18 during the showcase, and their stories should be under 10 minutes. When young storytellers feel ready to tell to a national audience, they can check the timeline and deadlines their state has for selecting state finalists. The NYSS committee tries to find a state chairperson to host or find youth participating in storytelling events in each state. Those state chairs are listed on the nationalyouthstorytellingshowcase.org website. If there is no state chair for their state, the youth teller can apply online at www.timpfest.org. The chairperson can designate up to five strong youth tellers annually to represent their state via video entry to the National Youth selection process.

The National Youth Storytelling event is no longer a competition but a celebration of these national finalists, showcasing their talents. Truly, the science and art of storytelling can be more effectively promoted among preadult communicators without competition at the final level. Youth tellers at the NYSS are reviewed and evaluated in learning skills, performing, and gaining ambassadorship skills. They can then be recommended to festivals and libraries back in their communities.

The original designation of torchbearer is still given as a title to finalists. The National Youth finalists used to be judged at the event. Now judging takes place prior to families deciding if they should raise money to travel or send their torchbearer to Utah to participate in the NYSS. A national selection committee determines who will receive the opportunity to tell. Identities are kept private in order to keep the integrity of their choices. Judging is subjective, and by allowing a judge to make up his or her own mind, without the influence of others, there is a natural break in scores where all judges select the same top 7–10 state finalists.

Those who travel to Utah are named torchbearers for the next year, to act as storytelling ambassadors in their communities. They are instructed to hold the torch of storytelling high so their flame can light the way, teach others to share their stories, and nurture other storytellers to enjoy the same success. As they build others through story, they will build and connect their communities.

Some torchbearers have returned home and have actively participated in coaching other youth, performing, and finding storytelling opportunities for themselves and others. The National Youth Storytelling events make a difference in lives. They go home changed, with a new awareness and determination to serve others in their communities.

One torchbearer enjoyed his time in Utah and was determined to come back the very next year. When he arrived home, he looked at the charge to be an ambassador for storytelling in his area, talked with his amazing teacher who had also attended, and began helping her coach other youth tellers. He passed the torch instead of returning himself.

There have been several youth who tried year after year without receiving a final invitation. Some even traveled all the way to Utah to participate in events and attend without performing. They also took the charge to keep trying, keep telling, and encourage others. Some have returned as strong storytellers being named torchbearers at last.

While in Utah, the torchbearers meet and forge an almost instant bond. They play together and then are prepared to learn together in an environment of trust. The youth storytellers tell at the NYSS soon after they arrive. Without competition, the families seem free to laugh and cheer for each other. They are invited to attend a day and a half of Timpanogos Storytelling Conference classes. Torchbearers participate in team-building activities. They attend Timpanogos Storytelling Festival performances and are each invited to tell on the Timpanogos Storytelling stages. Timpanogos has built a legacy of placing young tellers before almost every hour of professional storytelling performances. Young and well-seasoned tellers blend the program as they tell together.

A favorite event at NYSS is the storyteller Q&A where torchbearers are up close and personal with working storytellers. The youth are encouraged to bring questions they may have, to learn anything from how to handle a forgetful moment on stage to what life is like as a working performing artist. This further connection of storytellers, young with experienced, offers a shepherding for the young tellers. Their questions and opinions are valued and validated by those who have gone before and create an opportunity for mentors to develop.

The benefits of storytelling and skills gained reach far beyond the art itself. Young people can develop valuable skills of leadership, build confidence, and increase scholarship appeal and opportunities while gaining talent that cannot be found elsewhere. Not every participant will desire or find a career in storytelling. Whether the classroom or the boardroom is in their future, the skills gained from the NYSS program are unsurpassed.

Whatever the field a young person dreams of entering as he or she grows up, participating in the NYSS can help train him or her for it. NYSS participation will give an edge to anyone in any field. Timpanogos Storytelling gathers the top presenters in education, business, and storytelling. Young tellers will learn from the best. Presenting and performing skills can be improved through NYSS training and community building. Storytelling will grow with more youth learning, appreciating and preserving the age-old art. Storytelling grows as the audience for storytelling grows.

Imagine being able to learn and hone these skills at a young age. The possibilities are endless.

Heritage Night: School Programming

Jane Stenson

Currently, I am a storytelling teaching artist in the Mineral Point, Wisconsin, schools. The Senior Tax Exempt Program (STEP) indirectly funds my local work by reducing my property taxes! One has to be 55 and accepted by the school administration in order to participate. Having the school district and government working together to get literacy artists and mathematicians into the schools to enrich students is a wonderful model. Because I am retired and wish to give back to my community, this is an ideal way to work part-time with children and storytelling. Here is a description of one project in the elementary school.

October

The fourth-grade teacher—my cooperating teacher—telephoned, saying the new principal wanted the fourth grade to have a family evening, themed Heritage Night, in the spring to celebrate the diverse heritages of the people of Mineral Point and to celebrate our town's history.

"I want to offer something special. Let's be ambitious, each student will tell a story. Well, at best they'll all do some research about their family, and some will craft that research into a story that we'll tape and project for everyone to enjoy."

She did not want to cancel the general storytelling experience for all fourth graders; rather she wanted an add-on that a self-selected group of students would *tell* a personal family narrative.

And that was the beginning: general work with every fourth grader in the fall, in groups of 15–18 for six 45-minute sessions so that everyone had the speaking and listening experience provided through a traditional "learning to tell a story" residency.

Mid-January

I began in earnest with a (motivated) group of 16 students. Heritage Night was set for mid-April—three months to research and craft and learn to tell a family narrative: a luxury! The school has a built-in WIN (What I Need) time —or enrichment program—for all students, and for me that meant once-a-week half hour in the Library Media Center (LMC). When I teach storytelling, it is important for me to not be the sole expert in the room; rather I seek to develop a troupe or community of tellers who use critical thinking skills about language, about ideas bigger than the specifics of the story, and about compassion/support for the characters in the story and for themselves. Envision that each of the following *activities* takes as much time as it needs.

On Your Feet Telling a Folktale

This was review, but I wanted them to remember:

- how much fun they had as tellers and listeners;
- how the folktale structure helps them remember the story;
- how the story is about the character's journey—every detail serves the character's journey; and

- well-defined story elements constitute an enjoyable storytelling experience for teller and listener.

Personal Object Story

I asked students to find something in their home that was meaningful for their family. I asked them to ask family members—grandparents, parents, uncles, and aunts—maybe it is something great-grandmother brought here when she settled; maybe it is a war story; maybe it is something beautiful; or maybe some machinery. Find some *thing* to talk about with your family.

Here are some anecdotes about this initial "research," or looking for a nugget to begin the process of writing a family narrative, the gems from which the stories will be built. Forming the questions for the oral interviews comes later.

Charlie said he could bring a picture of the tractor. He and his dad and grandpa went to the barn where the tractor is parked. Charlie asked, "Why did you restore this tractor? You never use it; you keep it in the barn." Turns out this was a tractor from the 1940s—a small tractor in contrast to today's Big Agriculture, so prevalent around southwest Wisconsin. Charlie returned to class saying "Why did I ever ask them? They talked on and on. I know more about that tractor than I ever wanted to know."

And I wondered how I could help, knowing so little about tractors; as it developed, Charlie's story was set in the context of organic farming versus Big Agriculture.

Maya brought in a small pink tunic that her grandfather brought home from Vietnam. Smiling broadly, she held it up to show everyone: "He calls it Nam, not Vietnam. He liked the people so much, he wanted to bring back something of the people, not something of the war."

Her grandfather guarded the officers' compound in Saigon and did not participate in the jungle/guerrilla warfare.

Bryce's war story differed, and he brought in great candid photos of one of his great-grandfathers as a jeep driver in France during World War II. Both great-grandfathers died recently—one in late 2015 and the one about whom his story would be written died in January 2016. He wanted to remember his grandfather, so he wanted to write a story about him. I was concerned; his teacher was concerned. Bryce cried more than once during this process and eventually was able to place the World War II record as a staff jeep driver into a story that celebrated the long and family-oriented life of a loving great-grandfather, who returned home to the family farm after World War II.

Ella remembered her grandmother making *kringle*. She remembered the smells of the dough, from the oven, and from the *kringle* cooling on the counter. And she remembered her grandmother full of flour and sugar and hugs, and the grandkids (including her) running from the living room to the kitchen when it came out of the oven.

Tobin tried to write about the old sewing machine. Then he tried the lace tablecloth. Then he lamented, "I really want to do this. I want to tell a story and I can't find anything interesting. My mother keeps suggesting things, but these are things she likes. I don't want to write about a lace tablecloth."

Eventually, he wrote about the family's migration from Norway to America, finishing with a flourish: "...and that is why we are no longer Norwegians, instead we are Americans!"

February and March

The Big Questions

What is the story about? What is the setting and what is the big idea (theme) you are sharing? As a group (established as a peer review), we broke their ideas into basic story elements and developed these outside the story context.

Peer review pulls students from their solitary wrestling into a group where students notice and comment on specifics about another student's work. It allows students a way to practice the skills that matter in the telling of a story. It also creates compassion for the other students; each is as invested in her own story as well as the other stories. Students "know" the other's story—the struggle of the main character, the family history that causes our present-day lives.

- Does the listener have enough/too much information? Does the plot make sense?
- Choice of words that convey meaning, particularly active verbs
- Can you see the character—the hair, the dress, the straight back, the tight lips, the chewed off fingernails—images that visually project the character?

Step by Step

- Research (library and Internet) about setting—particularly for the immigration and war stories. We "envisioned" setting or place using Carol Birch's *Whole Story Handbook*: *Using Imagery to Complete the Story Experience* (August House, 2000).
- Developed sensory images of the setting
- Then a timed writing on their story's setting
- I asked, "Why is your story important in the long run scheme of things?" This was difficult! Asking fourth graders to put their specific character into a universal, historical context and somehow saying something significant about Big Agriculture, war, or immigration are working on the development of critical thinking. My approach was to offer a series of specific-to-universal as well as universal-to-specific exercises so the students could practice this skill and apply it to their story development.
- Plot: Sequentially, what happens in the story? A story is NOT a description; rather the character is faced with a dilemma and moves to solve it.

April

Telling the Story

In school, these students write but do very little in terms of speech, and nothing in storytelling. They greeted this piece of the process with nervousness and terror. Remembering these are good students, they overpracticed, and as much as I said, "*Don't memorize*, tell me your story as though we were sitting on the back porch," that did not happen for several weeks.

Step by Step

- I asked each student to create a six-framed storyboard and then tell their story to the wall.
- Students were directed: "*Tell* your story to two people you like. Have them give appreciations and ask questions."
- Several students did not want appreciations; they wanted critical comments so they could make the story better. That engendered a discussion, with me taking the lead on the value of appreciation and gratitude!
- I counseled the students to tell pieces of the story to their parents, relatives, the dog, and the goldfish, *explaining* that they must feel the words inside their mouths and watch how the "audience" hears the story. "What part did the dog like best?" is a great conversation starter for fourth graders, because it shows them immediately how much effect they produce.
- We practiced tricks to lessen the nerves such as gripping hands and shaking them so vigorously that you think you might stumble. We practiced vocal warm-ups (particularly humming) to move the air from the diaphragm to the front of the mouths. Do you feel the buzz in the front of your mouth? We practiced breathing techniques so their full breath could be used to support the story.

Filming

Another cause for nerves! I love working with highly motivated, smart students. Yet, they can be difficult (tightly wired) in their search for perfection! The LMC was the spot, and the librarian set up a backdrop and her computer. Cooperation with the librarian among and between the fourth-grade teachers, me, and the students was paramount. She filmed them on iPad using the DoInk app, which allowed her to play with the background(s). Then she used the iMovie app to put the entirety together.

I had said, "No notes," but several students made clever posters with outlines and word clues to prop next to the computer; so they looked at the camera and had the verbal prop. Nevertheless, most students made at least two attempts, and one had five! The librarian's patience—she likes this group—was highly supportive.

Mid-April: Heritage Night

The three fourth-grade classes and their families and some grandparents (especially of the storytellers!) arrived. The evening included general group presentations because every student presented something, such as:

- with a large group—sing some songs, act in an immigration play
- with a small group—several poems, some rap, cooking demonstrations, artworks, visual, pottery, weaving, knitting (this town has many artists whose children go to the school), interspersed with the storytellers' films. They were so well received! The town had no experience with storytelling, so curiosity was high. Families wanted to hear this troupe, probably because they had had a hand in the

creation of the story one way or another. The *stories* (and the students) did not disappoint their community. Initially, I wanted the students to tell the stories live, but the teachers convinced me that that was too much pressure. I swallowed and deferred. The projections of these smiling, fresh-faced, earnest tellers caused laughter, tears, and memories. The nerves did not show on film. Three and a half months of successful work!

The fourth-grade community consisting of the students, their extended families, and their teachers was delighted with the tellers. Storytelling is a *new* skill in the school. Having students articulate something of importance from their family history was a compliment beyond measure. When Bryce told his story of his grandfather and finished with "My great-grandpa died February 29th, 2016," there was a gasp that he had managed this story in so short a time. Then he added with a smile, "You understand that in four years on February 29th, 2020, he will have been dead for one year." A chuckle spread through the room. He demonstrated the first rule of great storytelling: "take your audience on a journey and be sure to bring them back."

The community of Mineral Point, composed of its many parts—the artistic community, the financial community, the farming community, to name a few—loves its children, who come together daily in the schools. The children live the different points of view stemming from these subcommunities. The magic of articulating those histories and differences into stories gathered the adults into the storytelling culture. In some ways, Mineral Point is based on an oral culture—everybody talks about everybody (gossip). But storytelling raises the way people are discussed—there is a higher purpose because we worked so hard on "What is your story about?" in order to reach a universal understanding of our common humanity. There were so many exchanges in the complimenting (appreciations) of one family to another, of students to students, of parents to teachers. Remember the teacher's charge. "I want to offer something special. Let's be ambitious!"

Well, *we* did it!

Bibliography

Birch, Carol. *Whole Story Handbook*: *Using Imagery to Complete the Story Experience*. Little Rock, AR: August House, 2000.

5

Voices of the Disenfranchised

*A powerful way to cross the bridge from outsider to insider is
to tell a story.*

—Dr. Indre Viskontas, Cognitive Neuroscientist

Editors' Comments

*If you have a strong purpose in life, you don't have to be pushed.
Your passion will drive you there.*

—Roy Bennett

Purpose and passion are the two distinguishing characteristics of the contributors in this chapter. Each of these inspiring storytellers has a deep passion for sharing stories that reach the hearts and minds of uniquely challenged—and challenging—populations.

Following the path of the Hero's Journey, these storytellers have heeded the "call to adventure," entered an "extraordinary world," encountered myriad obstacles and not-so-mythical helpers along the way, and have emerged transformed. But the most significant transformation is in their audience: isolated individuals have made connections and forged community, "cross[ing] the bridge from outsider to insider"—by telling their story.

Every journey presents its own set of challenges and trials, but these intrepid storyteller heroes are ready and willing to become your mentor on your own quest, sharing insights that will light your path and lighten your burden.

Crossroads: Stories for Reaching At-Risk Youth

Lorna MacDonald Czarnota

"Storyteller, tell me a story I can hold." I had already been working with at-risk youth for several years when a 15-year-old girl at the runaway shelter spoke those words.

Sometimes it is very easy to do what I do—reach this population of youth between ages 12 and 21 through the art of storytelling. At other times, it has been troubling, a struggle, heart wrenching, and even dangerous.

I have worked with thousands of at-risk youth since 1995 when it all began with a call to my family and I discovered my 16-year-old niece had been missing for two weeks. I had heard all the things that could happen to innocent young girls on unfamiliar streets, and by the time that journey ended, my niece had mirrored many of them, but she survived.

I began to question what we did wrong as a family, and since she did survive, I also asked what we did right. It all came down to exactly that—family. We were there for her regardless of what she did. We held her up and kept her in the fold. But not all of "my kids" have family. So for them, family is the community they create. We need to be part of that, a member of their family, so we can guide them. Long before my niece was safe, I realized how important it is for the community at large to grasp these youths in their arms. While I sought other ways in which to help, I took the journey with her. Prior to all this, I lived a sheltered life. I had no idea what was out there beyond the six o'clock newscast.

Scared out of my mind for my niece's well-being, I somehow (now, long forgotten) found my way to the door of Compass House, a local runaway shelter. I spoke with the director, seeking information on how to cope with my own emotions, how to help my niece, and what to do with a family that was torn between whether to help her or cast her aside out of disappointment. I have also long forgotten exactly when or how the director—my mentor and today my friend—asked me to work with the kids in their facility. That was in 1995 and at the time of this book, I am still there twice a month. Even though they can no longer pay me as they did in the beginning, the work is too important, and the kids are too important. They are "us" in a short time and to abandon them is to abandon humanity. I truly believe this.

As far as I knew, nobody else was doing anything similar. I was alone with a clean slate on which to write, and at the same time, no other storytellers to consult. But I was taking this journey out of a need and out of a passion. I made it up as I went. It is a "calling."

That early program had two components: visiting the shelter and running a coffeehouse at their resource center. As such, there were two goals: give the kids a voice, and give the kids some peace in their troubled world. These have expanded to include addressing issues and teaching life lessons, with the design of creating connections as we go.

The Resource Center was serving many of Western New York's teens by helping them with financial assistance, helping them find jobs and places to live, and locating the mental and emotional services they might require. The shelter was just a temporary home for kids in need, no matter where they came from. So, kids from the shelter went to the center, but the youth getting resources might no longer be, or never have been, at the house. There was crossover at times.

The kids who came to the coffeehouse heard me tell a couple of stories, and then we had open mic and they could do whatever kind of performance they wanted to do. The place was theirs. I was just a catalyst. Situations where teens feel they have the reins make them feel most comfortable and open. In the teen years, kids want the autonomy of adulthood while still wanting the security of childhood. It is a delicate balance.

As with all things, change happens, and the woman working for Compass House who was my supporter for the coffeehouse decided to leave for another job. Without internal interest, the coffeehouse faded away, but the director knew my work by then and had seen results—reluctant kids who beamed when telling her about the event. So, with her foresight, I kept a "group" running, where an interested and often "captive audience" came to hear a story and do some activities around it, including artwork.

My goal in these five-session groups was to get them to tell their own stories, reflect back on what they heard, and connect the folk and fairytales with their own lives. This was when I discovered that they did so best through their art. The pictures they drew and the masks they made allowed them to "hide"—to be anonymous. This anonymity is crucial to their survival on the street. They cannot afford to let their guard down and wear their hearts on their sleeves. It is emotionally and physically dangerous for them to do so. And yet. And yet. And yet, they offer their hearts freely once trust is established. They just would not tell you that that is what they are doing.

The "group" is where I came in contact with the toughest kids—the most outwardly disruptive. But it was all a test. They learn to test everyone they come in contact with using their own brand of litmus, often disguised as outburst or sick humor. I am made of something, I do not know what to call it, but it allows me to be waterproof, resistant, like feathers on a duck. I never flinch. I have never run away. I have cried but only after I have gotten home, and not over what they have done or said, but because I know how deeply they hurt. I constantly search for ways to touch them. And because I have been stalwart, staying with them no matter what, like my family stayed with my niece, the toughest of kids have accepted me. More importantly though, through accepting me, they have heard what the stories have to say.

"Storyteller, tell me a story I can hold." This girl was just one of the many. I remember her name. It was Jessica. She sat quiet, almost asleep in a chair in the parlor at the shelter. The other kids that night were particularly boisterous and obnoxious. I do not "police" the kids. If they break house-rules, that is up to staff. I cannot afford to be "the bad guy." I have to be the "grandmother" who gives them dessert when they are supposed to eat their veggies. And while it is distracting if they are disruptive or loud, there are tools we use as storytellers, the same ones teachers use to overcome those outbursts. I know the magic of eye contact and proximity. I know how to use my voice and my silence to change behaviors. As for obnoxious, that is part of the process. Why would a teen who has been physically, emotionally, or mentally abused; called names; thrown out of the house; seen someone he or she cares about die; or any myriad of other horrors, trust and respect you, an outsider? You earn it. How? By giving of yourself and the gift of the story without expectation. You do not expect them to listen. You do not expect them to behave or accept or be kind. The reward is that they will. They will. Because you have given them what they need most—acceptance.

So, after all of that hard work, this teen girl who seemed to be asleep came up to me after we closed our circle and we were alone.

"Storyteller," she said.

"Yes," I replied, smiling.

"Tell me a story I can hold."

"What do you mean?"

"I need a story, Miss. My life is a mess. I miss home. I need a story."

And so, I took her to a chair, and in a darkened quiet corner, I sat next to her and told her a story all her own, just for her. What story? You know, I have long forgotten that as well, but it does not matter. I knew what she needed. She needed the gift of someone who would take some time to speak to her soul.

I may have forgotten exactly how this work started, but I remember why, and I will never forget kids like Jessica. Or Terrance, who created a picture of himself, holding his heart, with his head detached. Or Joey, a tough kid from out of town who gently held my four-month-old kitten and the lesson he taught me about prejudging others. Or the gang kid who sat on the bookcase and would not participate because, as he said, "It doesn't matter, Miss. I'll either be dead or in jail in six months."

I worked for nine years as the resident storyteller at a residential treatment facility until they closed, and I work yearly for eight weeks at a girls' group home. I continue my work at the shelter and have written three books about this journey. And although I may not be deeply entrenched in a regular position at a facility, every teen I come in contact with, and parents whose hearts are breaking, and communities whose children are dying, belong to me. In fact, they belong to all of us.

If you walk down the street and pass by a teen, do you look them in the eye and say, "Hello?" Or hold your purse a little tighter and cross the street?

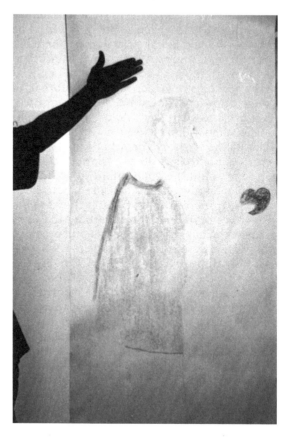

Terrance's Self-Portrait

I thought Joey was going to smash my kitten against the wall, but I promised the kids they could see her; so I opened her cage. He whisked her up and I began a litany of instructions on how to handle her. "I know, Miss," he said, "I have a cat at home and I miss her." He nuzzled her and then carried her around to all the other kids telling them, "Be careful, she's so little." What messages are we sending? What stories are we telling if we do not make contact?

As I said, there have been times this work is dangerous. I have sat beside murderers and never knew it at the time. I have been in places where kids could jump you. Does that scare me? Yes. You need awareness. But it must never get in the way of the gift of self if we want to truly change the world, one child at a time—my motto. Telling stories to at-risk youth is more about giving of self than it is about the story. That is why I can walk down a street after seeing a teen once and have him or her run after me for a hug while shouting, "Storyteller!" That is why a youth who has experienced my program tells the rest to "Shut up, man. She's real. Just Listen." And that is why I keep doing what I do and answering the call, even when the money does not follow. It is not a matter of wanting to do this. It is a matter of having to do this. We have to be part of the lives of these kids in our communities if we all wish to survive and thrive.

There are ways we can reach youth and create positive community through storytelling because the stories tell the truths many people do not necessarily want to know. I have heard kids just sigh or take in a deep breath after a hard story. Some have said, "Wow Miss, why did he do that," in response to character action. They get it. They do not need explanations.

When I ask them to tell their personal stories, we sometimes do them in third person so they have some distance from which to view character actions, and because I want them to realize that the folk and fairytales they hear are more than just stories. They speak to truth and their own experiences in life.

Finding opportunities for meaningful programs is not always easy, and getting paid can be even harder. Pay in a social work setting for ongoing programming has not been as lucrative as storytelling for a single program or a day in a school or library. In truth, if you can find situations that do pay well, it would be a rarity. My advice when talking to other storytellers who want to do this work is that it should not be for the sake of income. Certainly, if money is offered, take it. We have enough trouble in the mainstream convincing people to believe in what we do as artists.

I also advise storytellers to always "be real" with the kids. They see right through phony and will respect you more if you are yourself. Know that even being able to tell a five-minute story and simply be present with them makes ripples that turn into waves and are so important.

Some distance is necessary. You need to go in, do your work of telling stories, follow up with staff if any issues arise that might endanger them or the kids, and leave. Go home, kick the wall, and cry if you have to, but be safe—emotionally and physically. Do not try to break up fights. Do not offer rides if a youth asks, or money, or other requests—it happens. Be aware of your surroundings and open and vulnerable at the same time. I think this is the trickiest part of what we need to do, and it may require mentorship, practice, and lots of time to get there.

Show no fear. Be loving.

Where to Begin

As to where to find funding, or actual groups to work with, there are runaway shelters in many cities across the nation. More group homes and treatment centers are opening their doors. Boys and Girls Clubs and schools often have needy children. Offer to start programs for them, whether a single visit or five- to six-week programs. Churches are good venues as well, and some church groups offer small grants. Storytelling organizations also have occasional grants.

Whether you do this work for payment or not, you will need to approach facilities with a proposal. When will you come, for how long? What will you do? What fee would you like? How many kids can you handle in a group? What kind of venue do you need? You will need this information for grantors also.

Planning for Group Sessions

Teens are on the edge of becoming adults, and most at-risk youth have skipped a beat someplace, already experiencing adulthood well before their time. Do not shy away from the hard stories. In fact, if I ask the kids what they would like to hear, it is almost always "a scary story."

Always be prepared with a couple of stories. Maybe a scary one and something more quiet and simple, just in case. You never really know where the kids' heads will be. I always call the facility a couple hours before my program to get a head count, if I am doing an art project, and an idea what issues they might be dealing with. In more volatile populations, like those in treatment centers where they have sometimes experienced serious traumas, things can change quickly, even during a story. You need to be prepared to walk away. Or a teen may have to leave in the middle of a story, either due to behavior dangerous to his or her person or others, to be given meds, or because they have a phone call. Anything is possible.

I do try to encourage kids to stay and work through fears if we are working on a darker story. Not only is it important for them to work past fight-or-flight responses, but the imagination can make a story far darker than it is. Stories usually have a favorable resolution from which we learn a great deal. Kids who leave without that resolution can actually be extra traumatized. There have been times when I make sure that a young person gets to hear the end of the story, even if it means a solo performance.

I ended up spending a couple years taking courses at the university to be certified in trauma counseling. I am not legally able to call myself a counselor, but I verified my knowledge and added to it. This gave me more confidence, helped me speak the same language as the youth counselors, and gave agencies more confidence in me as well. Take every opportunity to learn about the population, treatments, and, of course, storytelling.

It is possible that you will tell stories for 10–30 minutes with small or large groups of teens, then never see them again, or they will show up elsewhere. Shelters are like this. The kids are very transient. You need to plan for that situation.

Let kids be where they need to be. I have had staff try to shake kids awake and tell them they are being rude by sleeping, and all that does is set up animosity. I believe in letting them sleep if they need to, and things get in the cracks. In fact, many times they are just pretending to sleep. They are controlling their environment.

I recently had one boy slouching with his eyes closed when I arrived. I stood in front of him, bent over, and said, "Hi. I'm here to tell a story."

He opened one eye and said, "Don't think I'm rude, but I'll probably be asleep."

"Okay," I said, "I never make kids stay awake. Sleep if you need to. Something will get in."

He sat up and did not slouch or fall asleep the whole time. Why?

"Because you tell good stories, Miss."

I smiled all the way home.

You can find group homes or treatment centers where kids are there for longer periods of time. Programs of six to eight weeks, meeting for one to two hours per week, work well in these settings. I keep my times flexible. Sometimes we can get a lot done and we go over; other times we may only need an hour.

Do not be discouraged if you are turned down by an agency. They can have legal restraints placed on them. Confidentiality is always paramount. Safety is important to everyone. At one point my programs at the treatment center were suspended due to a rash of incidents where kids injured staff members.

Remember you still make a difference if you look at a teen and smile. Tell stories at every opportunity. And do not forget, it is not about the story. It is about the caring and unconditional gift of self. The story opens the door, but nothing happens unless you and the listeners dare to go through it together.

The following is a sampling of one eight-session program outline from my book *Dancing at the Crossroads: A Guide for Practitioners in At-Risk Programming: Stories of Choice and Empowerment* (Parkhurst\Brothers, 2014). It focuses on stories that help youth make better choices and show them that no matter what happens in life, choices always exist. This in itself is empowering to the individual. Most Crossroads Story Center programs include a similar progression.

- Session One: Trust Building activities and stories to set the tone for the following sessions and begin forming relationships in a group.

- Session Two: Preevaluation and Discussion of Metaphor. Evaluation lets you know in advance what skills youth have. Understanding Metaphor helps them utilize healing stories throughout their lives.

- Session Three: Optional Icebreaker Game. Use a game designed to get the youth interactive with story. Story Cubes are one way to do this and game be purchased at book and toy stores.

- Session Four: Begin developing stories that the youth will write about themselves. Use third-person point of view or leading questions such as "When was a time you learned a valuable lesson?"

- Session Five: Share stories from session four.

- Session Six: Story and Art Activity. You can tell a story each week, but if you have not told one since the first session, do so now. The art activity will be based on the stories you want them to tell during the final session. Youth find it easier to tell a story if they can "hide" behind their art.

- Session Seven: This session is a continuation of session six if needed. You can also begin a second project, or fill the time with telling stories.

- Session Eight: Sharing youth stories and art. Invite staff and mentors. Rite of Passage Ceremony. Create a special event like a graduation.

You can change the world, one child at a time.

Bibliography

Czarnota, Lorna MacDonald. *Dancing at the Crossroads: A Guide for Practitioners in At-Risk Programming*: *Stories of Choice and Empowerment*. Marion, MI: Parkhurst Brothers, 2014.

The Power of Creative Story for Alzheimer's Patients and Those with Other Special Needs

Pete and Joyce Vanderpool

The witch said, "I'll get you, my pretty. You'll see what it is like to be a dog!" The witch took a limb from a magic tree and swirled it in the air, around and around her head. "You will have fur, your nose will be long and your ears pointed. You will have four legs and your tail will show your emotions." She pointed the limb at him and said, "From now on, you will be called Ronnie."

—Excerpt from *A Dog Story—With a Moral**

Makes you want to hear the rest of the story, doesn't it? Now consider that this is a portion of a story written by a group of high functioning adults with intellectual disabilities. Trousdale School is a special community of true friends who cheer each other along while always striving for excellence. Students are provided academics, life skills, and vocational training and placement for the purpose of becoming their most independent selves. While working together on this story during Creative Story Week, it was obvious that they took great pride in their story writing achievement. And the power of story was proven once again.

The development of the Story Power process started with a discussion on a National Storytelling Network (NSN) listserv for storytellers regarding Time*Slips* and their work with Alzheimer's and dementia patients in nursing homes. Creative Story Project's Story Power program is an expansion of the Time*Slips* process (http://www.timeslips.org/) developed by Dr. Anne Basting of the University of Wisconsin–Milwaukee through the Helen Bader School of Social Welfare. As certified facilitators of the program, we identified the benefits of the fun, creative group process that makes the art of oral storytelling accessible to sufferers of Alzheimer's and dementia by replacing the pressure to remember with the encouragement to imagine. The program provides many opportunities for positive interaction and great fun. Creative story creates improvement in the quality of relationships between staff and residents as well as resident to resident. An ongoing lively, stimulating, and energizing program can be transforming for the residents of facilities or those attending day care programs. The process is a form of behavioral or cognitive therapy, although we are not and do not profess to be therapists. We would encourage anyone working with Alzheimer's/dementia patients to consider using the Time*Slips* process and becoming a certified facilitator.

Our nonprofit corporation, Creative Story Project, utilizes the power of story as a learning tool or an agent of change for students of all ages. In addition to Alzheimer's/dementia patients, this includes those with learning challenges, at-risk youth, and the incarcerated. The Story Power program provides an environment where participants can flourish in an atmosphere that is accepting, respectful, nonjudgmental, and meaningful. Through the process of story creation by participants, the stage is set for creating positive interactions and increasing a sense of community. Creative story can cause an improvement in the quality of relationships within a group while providing an exciting exercise. Many of these benefits are more qualitative, not easily measured, but certainly readily visible.

> *Jethro is being a geek. He is very smart and kind of a nerd. He is six years old in dog years which is 42 in human years. He is trying to be a teacher so he is teaching math and is grading the math papers. He is teaching fourth and fifth grade but is working towards being a principal with his doctorate.*
> —Excerpt from *Professor Jethro Glasses Mann***

The same picture of dog with pencil used by a group of at-risk inner-city youth takes a totally different direction with the character striving for a better life. The process was the same; the outcome was totally different.

> *Bob Nerd is chewing on his pencil while he pays bills for his business. He is a millionaire business owner. He is a lawyer. His office is a dog penthouse that you get to through his dog house. His clients include Poodles, Yorkies, Chihuahuas, Pomeranians, Shih Tzus, and other kinds of dogs. His business clients include State Farm, Spectrum, Nationwide, and Game Stop. He has one cat client. His biggest competition is Poodle Insurance.*
> —Excerpt from *Mr. Bob's Business Adventures****

Again, the same picture used with a group of third- to fifth-grade students showed a desire for success and stature. This story became part of a 240-page book of story with each of 25 students contributing an 8-page chapter as part of the Cleveland City Schools (Tennessee) After School University Summer Program.

Potential collaborators and recipients for this type of program can include schools, Parent Teacher Associations and Parent Teacher Organizations, libraries, Boys and Girls Clubs, Big Brothers/Big Sisters, Girl Scouts, Boy Scouts, YMCA, church youth groups, local service agencies, juvenile or family court systems, or any organization that serves children and youth.

But it does not end here. The same process has also been used with incarcerated women. Locked behind steel doors, offenders are left with the story of what was, and a bleak story of the now. A story that tells about tomorrow does not resonate in their ever-fading imagination. Through the use of Story Power and its creative story techniques, women can focus on learning to see what can be true outside the walls of prison, giving hope for life upon release.

A black and white photo of two kids play-fighting on a sandy beach ended up with inmates seeing brilliant blue-green waves, colorful mermaids, and a calming visualization of where to go mentally when conflict arises. The stories created push the women to reframe the way they think about their ability to grasp hope and create options.

These options for the women vary for different situations. They relate to dealing with conflict in their secure but crowded location. But they begin to move their thinking beyond the walls as women apply the stories to their family situations and the hope they have for change when they get out. When temptation arises, they have learned some concepts that make them realize other options are available. They are no longer stuck with the way it has always been.

These women are becoming artists of oral storytelling. They have a role, a place, value, and a story. As stories are heard and told, compassion and confidence grow. Story brings light into a dark place and gives hope.

The process for all these groups is fairly simple and easy to grasp by storytelling "professionals" and novices alike. The facilitators present specially selected photographs around which the group collaboratively weaves a fictional tale. The resulting creation is written down by the facilitators, transcribed and returned to the creators both orally and in written form. Pictures are carefully selected to be nonthreatening and noncontroversial. As a result they often include children or animals in funny situations. Care must be taken to only select pictures that are uncopyrighted or royalty free, or taken by someone you know who gives permission for their use. If pictures are found on the Internet, permission should be requested or payment should be made for the image. Colored pictures work best, although that does not preclude the use of black and white or sepia tones.

Before starting each session, we ask that each participant has a name tag with just his or her first name. This serves two purposes: (1) we can call them by name, an important facet of the program, and (2) by collecting the tags at the end of the session, we have a record of the participants to add to the story. This information is added at the bottom of the transcribed story along with the location, date, and any credits necessary. Last names are not used.

Two facilitators (or one with an assistant) are necessary—one to guide the questions and answers, and the other to act as scribe, writing responses on a flip chart for later transcription. Using the tried and true process of storytelling, the participants will name the characters, decide on things like the location, time, or weather, have three "problems" if possible, supply a solution, and come to a suitable ending. Quite often the title of the story comes after it is completely written, but if it comes sooner, write it down! And remember, there is no such thing as a wrong answer! If two or three different answers come at the same time, they can usually be sorted out or used in a different way. For example, when naming a character, if one person says "Elsie" and another one wants "Claire," ask them if they think Elsie can be the first name and Claire the middle name. Or if they are trying to figure out what kind of dog is pictured, be prepared to make it a mutt, or if it is obviously a poodle, ask one of the staff to "break the tie."

It is important to stop periodically and read back the story as it develops. Participants may have forgotten what was said or may want to do some editing. For instance, once while working on a story about a small child and his burro, the beginning said the child thought he wanted a dog for his birthday but got a burro instead. However, the closing line supplied by a resident was so dynamic, "Dad, let's go to Wal-Mart and get me a bicycle," that the group changed the beginning from a dog to a bicycle. It was their choice and made a better story.

Group size should be kept to 10 or fewer if at all possible to allow for the greatest amount of interaction and personal attention possible. When working with Alzheimer's patients or persons with learning challenges, personnel from the facility and family members should be present to assist since often they will better understand the responses of the participants. About 45 minutes should be set aside for each story. And the facilitator(s) should return to the facility each week at the same time for a period of 8–10 weeks (or two to three times a week if better for scheduling), taking copies of the previous week's story with them for presentation and distribution.

Constantly lavish praise and thanks to the contributors while encouraging others to participate. Sometimes one participant will prod another to give an answer. Encourage that action, but do not push the nonparticipant into a position of discomfort or fear.

Above all else, make it fun! Be involved! Be enthusiastic! Remember there is no "wrong" answer. If the story goes astray or comments and answers become inappropriate, bring the discussion back as quickly as possible to the picture and the story so far. This is a good time to break and reread the story in progress, bringing their thinking back to the task at hand.

To better understand your audience and potential special requirements they may have, be knowledgeable about them. Study, read, join organizations, and make yourself the best possible presenter you can be. For Alzheimer's work, we highly recommend the Alzheimer's Foundation of America of which we are members. The NSN is always a valuable resource. Librarians (both school and public) are valuable resources. Be smart. Be trained. Be accomplished. And always be joyful about the work you are doing.

Materials Needed

- 8.5 × 11 sheets with "silly" picture, preferably in color, enough for each participant. To save money, collect pictures at the end of session. Having the pictures in plastic sheet protectors is effective to reuse them for use in future programs.
- Colored markers. Possibly ask participants what the color of the day is.
- Name tags, plain white labels by the sheet are fine.
- Flip chart of plain white paper. (Note: to save money, our local newspaper donates end rolls of newsprint, which we cut into appropriate size sheets and clamp to an empty flip chart backing.)

A Word about Compensation

For the independent person wishing to pursue this program, compensation is sometimes difficult. Nursing homes usually only have about $100/month for "entertainment." However, although this program has an entertainment value, it really is a therapy or educational program. It is possible that a nursing home or assisted living facility can place it in a different line item in their budget. Schools may have a budget to fit it into reading or writing classes. Any nonprofit organization can be encouraged to write a grant to cover your expense, which we suggest as being $100/week to cover time, materials, and transportation.

If you are a nonprofit corporation, you will be able to find grants available for most schools or special-needs students, but not as readily for nursing homes. In searching for these grants, you must be able to prove the value of the program in advance and be ready to report on your success at the end of it. Although most results are qualitative, good records can provide quantitative results. Keep a chart of participants' names and attendance and notes about their participation with anecdotes about specific "happenings." Corporate sponsors are also a possibility.

Enjoy the Full Stories

*A Dog Story—with a Moral

This dog is really a boy named Ronald. He was turned into a dog by a witch. Here's how it happened.

A witch put a spell on him and changed him into a dog because he was not being nice to dogs and doing things like throwing rocks at them.

One day Ronald was throwing rocks at a dog and chased it into the woods. A witch appeared and said, "Hey, Stop that! That's my dog!"

But Ronald kept throwing rocks and teasing the dog. He answered the witch, "I don't have to do that." And he threw another rock.

The witch said, "I'll get you, my pretty. You'll see what it is like to be a dog!"

The witch took a limb from a magic tree and swirled it in the air, around and around her head. "You will have fur, your nose will be long and your ears pointed. You will have four legs and your tail will show your emotions." She pointed the limb at him and said, "From now on, you will be called Ronnie."

Now the only thing that lets you know that Ronnie used to be the boy named Ronald was that he was still wearing his glasses. But the witch said, "You will be human again when you learn how a dog feels when it's being mistreated." And with that, she disappeared.

Ronnie walked home where he saw his cat Mittens. The cat hissed at him and Ronnie said, "What's wrong? Don't you recognize me?" So Ronnie ran into the house thinking that Mittens must just be in a bad mood.

When he got in the house he found some papers and a pencil on the floor where someone had left them. He wrote on the paper, "Don't worry—it's me."

About then his family came home and finding a dog in the house, they shooed him out. Now Ronnie knew what being chased felt like. But outside he saw a big dog named Peter who said, "Hey! What happened?" So Ronnie told him about being chased out of the house. He didn't understand why they chased him away. But Peter explained that they did that because dogs don't belong in the house.

Ronnie had learned his lesson so he went to find the dog he had chased and hit with stones, and he apologized. The witch suddenly appeared with her magic stick. The witch spoke and understood dog language, so she said, "Did you learn your lesson, Ronnie?" "Yes I did," replied Ronnie, also speaking dog language.

The witch raised her magic limb and waved it over Ronnie, and he suddenly became the boy Ronald. Then she disappeared.

The moral of the story is "Treat animals like a friend."

**Professor Jethro Glasses Mann

Jethro is being a geek. He is very smart and kind of a nerd. He is six years old in dog years which is 42 in human years. He is trying to be a teacher so he is teaching math and is grading the math papers. He is teaching fourth and fifth grade but is working towards being a principal with his doctorate.

He teaches at E. L. Ross. The pencil in his mouth is used to write the answers he gets from his calculator. He has 15 students in each of two math classes and 19 students in his chemistry class.

When he is done, he will give the papers back to the students to write an essay about Chihuahuas. The essays will be graded by his partner, the president of the school whose name is Dr. Fred Harry.

After work, Jethro sits on the couch watching TV and eating hamburgers with Coke and a bone for dessert. He is watching Rocket Science but also enjoys Sponge Bob and Elmo. On Saturday, he watches Bill Nye the Science Guy and sometimes even some cartoons.

Jethro is asking his owner who adopted him to sharpen his pencil. As a hobby Jethro has made machines, a pencil sharpener, robots, calculators and mechanical pencils. He warns people not to put the mechanical pencil in the pencil sharpener.

Jethro lives in a dog mansion where he has lived for two years. He bought the materials and had it built. It is 10 feet long, 60 feet wide and 11 feet high. It is built of birch wood with bone trim. The mansion has a gym for exercise, a race track and a football field in the back yard. He has a butler and a bunch of friends. One day a month, Jethro goes to the pound and brings all the dogs home to play in his yard. When they go back to the pound, they have had a happy day.

***Mr. Bob's Business Adventures

Bob Nerd is chewing on his pencil while he pays bills for his business. He is a millionaire business owner. He is a lawyer. His office is a dog penthouse that you get to through his dog house. His clients include Poodles, Yorkies, Chihuahuas, Pomeranians, Shih Tzus, and other kinds of dogs. His business clients include State Farm, Spectrum, Nationwide, and Game Stop. He has one cat client. His biggest competition is Poodle Insurance.

He is looking out the window until his next client comes in. He is then going to talk to his new client, Phil the Turtle, who is suing someone that ran him over. Steve is his next appointment and he is a robot designer. Steve is already a client who is being sued because someone said he stole their ideas.

George, a new client, got stuck in glue chasing a robber who turned out to be Bob's girlfriend. Bob is sending George to another lawyer named Sherry the Penguin. And now Bob is thinking about lunch. He isn't sure if he is going to have pizza, hot dogs, or lobster. He's going to take them all to lunch at "Bone" Appétit so he can talk to them. Bob saves the day!

Storytelling in the Addiction Recovery Community

Gene and Peggy Helmick-Richardson

Recalling how her apartment had what she called the "homeless" smell, B. recounts how she tolerated the stream of so-called friends who crashed in her bedroom, stole her personal belongings, dealt drugs from her living room, and eventually locked her out.

H. questions why his father singled him out of all the children in the family for abuse, and R. reminisces about a love lost due to expectations that could not be met because of addiction. A. laments how her parents deceived her into signing what she thought were guardianship papers so they could enroll her son for health insurance; it was weeks later when she discovered that what she had signed were adoption papers. Driven to prostitution to buy her drugs, S. warns others that one of her johns deliberately infected her, as well as other women, with the HIV virus.

These stories inspire others in the room to share their tales. Far too many of these accounts have scenarios in common—childhood predators, sexual abuse, domestic violence, attempted suicides, and so on.

Despite the frustration, anger, and tragedy of the stories, each teller aims to end his or her account on a positive note. These storytellers have survived addiction and are now clean and sober and struggling to stay that way. As part of their own healing, they are inspired to help others in the addiction community through one of the time-honored traditions—telling their personal story of recovery.

Meeting every Monday night in a Spartan room at Homeward Bound, a treatment center in the North Oak Cliff neighborhood of Dallas, the usually 20–30 participants are there voluntarily. The majority here are residents in the treatment facility, some are graduates of the program, and a few are here because they have friends who attend and urge them to come as well.

Our goal is for each member to learn how to share their own story so that others will listen and be inspired by it. These participants will also hear the stories of others in recovery and take the lessons in those accounts to advance their own recovery process.

How this storytelling program, partially funded through a Texas Commission on the Arts grant, came to be is a demonstration of perseverance, determination, and a love of storytelling. Not only on our part but that of the Homeward Bound staff and clients as well.

Although primarily making our living as storytellers for schools, libraries, and community organizations, we have a passion for sharing stories in therapeutic environments. We enjoy seeking out and telling stories that may advance one or more healing processes—be it physically, emotionally, or spiritually. Since 1999, we have shared stories in an assortment of service or therapeutic locales, including family violence shelters, homeless refuges, hospice programs, medical facilities (a children's hospital and a cancer treatment center), prisons (county, state, and federal), and Homeward Bound Inc., a nonprofit dedicated to treating those with substance abuse issues and mental illness, particularly for the indigent.

It is our work with the clients at Homeward Bound that has proved to be our most rewarding endeavor and, despite its totally unplanned beginnings, the work here has led to surprisingly unexpected and successful outcomes.

In 1995, Gene met Doug Denton, the cofounder and director of Homeward Bound, and casually mentioned that he was a storyteller. Doug asked if he could come tell to the clients. At that time, the residential facility was in a converted home just south of downtown Dallas that housed 18 adults, both male and female. That request turned into monthly evening visits from Gene. At that time, Peggy was not yet storytelling, but she would occasionally come along just to listen to the stories and support the program. Although the initial purpose of these storytelling programs was for pleasant diversion for the clients, an emphasis was placed on those inspirational and life-affirming tales that would promote a drug-free, alcohol-free lifestyle. It soon became evident that the stories were having a positive influence on these men and women struggling to beat addiction. Counselors reported that the clients shared the stories during later individual and group sessions, and those clients who returned to the center because of relapse often requested specific stories that had been told during their previous treatment period—often several years earlier. We even personally witnessed a storytelling session ending with two clients—one an African American man and the other an outspoken skinhead who had been at combative odds for several weeks—taking steps to share their personal stories as a way of understanding each other and sealing that commitment with a hug.

Within a few years, the center purchased and renovated an old osteopathic hospital—exploding into a five-floor, 120-bed facility. With the extra space, Homeward Bound added new services, including a detox ward and separate areas for the male and female clients. Gene started telling twice a month, once in the Men's Unit and again in the Women's Unit. In 1999, a very reticent Peggy finally screwed up the courage to join Gene in telling stories.

Over the years, the state of Texas whittled financial assistance down to the point where a once 90-day treatment program had to be compacted into a two-week program. What that meant for our program was that since we were going twice a month, once for the men and once again for the women, over half of the clients never heard us tell stories. And those who did get to participate had only one storytelling session.

The obvious solution was for us to come more often, but that was a luxury that we could not financially afford at that time—and with the growing addiction population and an ancient physical infrastructure, every penny that came into Homeward Bound was already spoken for. Even in the most generous of communities, donating to drug addiction causes generally hits near the bottom of most donors' lists. Of course, we could have peddled our services to for-profit drug treatment centers, but that did not feel right. For years, we had witnessed so many wonderful people struggling to overcome their addictions in a society that treats both drug use and poverty as a crime. Telling Homeward Bound we were going somewhere else because they could not afford us was just wrong.

While we were wrestling with this quandary, Homeward Bound was working with innovative programs to aid its clients and test out potential treatment protocols. One that proved to be a keeper was its 60-day residential Statewide program, serving clients who were also HIV+. Because of the HIV+ diagnosis, the state not only provides the additional funding but also offers extensions for up to 90 days. Many of the employees for the new program had transferred from the Men's and Women's Units and began asking if we could come tell there as well. As is often the case, we did not see the solution right before our eyes. Instead we declined because we did not have enough time as it was.

It took us a couple of years before the obvious smacked us upside the head. Why not tell for the Statewide clients instead of the clients in the Men's and Women's Unit? But telling here also provided new challenges—the biggest was identifying a time to tell that would fit around the other activities during the day. Was there a block of time when most of the clients could attend on a regular basis, a time when they were not with their counselors, standing in line for medications, or participating in other experimental programs such as determining the benefits of exercise for patients who are HIV+?

After several years of schedule juggling, it was determined that Monday mornings worked best for the clients, staff, and us. Monday morning storytelling bookings were pretty much nonexistent. The time proved so convenient for everyone that we soon found coming every Monday morning was easily doable.

Today we work with most of the Statewide clients for seven to eight weekly programs, so they come to know us well and greet us enthusiastically when we arrive. The harried staff expresses genuine appreciation for what we do—at the very least, we give them an hour-and-a-half to get paper work done, and at best our stories help their clients see addiction as well as life in general, in different ways. In addition, the stories often provide a reference point for discussing issues in new ways during individual and group counseling sessions.

Often addiction is a symptom of deeper problems and the result of self-medicating to alleviate the pain or suppress the suffering. So once the grip of physical addiction is weakened by detoxification, the psychological problems previously masked by the drugs and alcohol are able to be addressed. Homeward Bound counselors do this primarily through Cognitive Behavior Therapy, a form of psychotherapy that addresses emotions, thoughts, and behaviors and how they influence each other.

To reinforce this therapy, many of our stories focus on the conscious choices the characters make that often lead to unexpected consequences. We also tell tales from a variety of cultures that address the spiritual reasons for our human existence. We urge the clients to "follow your bliss" and contribute their own unique gifts to the world. Many of the stories we select are classic hero/heroine tales from an array of cultures (from Arthurian legends and *Grimms' Fairy Tales* to Greek, Roman, and Chinese mythology) and wisdom tales from an array of spiritual traditions (Buddhist, Sufi, Christian, etc.) that empower the listener to step forward in faith and trust in their abilities to see them through their quest. An assortment of trickster tales (Coyote, Anansi, Rabbit) offers a lighthearted warning about the choices we make.

Our greatest satisfaction comes when we are approached on the street by past clients who recount their favorite stories and share how their recovery is going. A treasured and unexpected gift was given to us one evening while out celebrating our wedding anniversary. Coming out of the theater, we heard someone yell, "Hey Storytellers!" A man rushed up to us, reached in his pocket, and showed us a stone. "I've kept this with me ever since you gave it to me two years ago and I've been clean for over two years now. And I want to thank you." After an exchange of hugs and congratulations, he disappeared into the crowd, but his success and the validation of the stories stay with us still.

And the point of the stone? A basket of rocks is an integral part of our storytelling programs at Homeward Bound.

Upon arrival, Peggy does all the necessary signing in, while Gene heads to the meeting room to get the chairs in a circle and set up a shrine of sorts in the middle of the room. The items on this focal point are significant to us and symbolize a variety of spiritual beliefs, including several that reflect Gene's Cherokee roots. In the center of this is a candle representing a campfire. Gene points out to the group that this candle also serves to unite us to our ancestors who were the first to sit around a fire and tell stories.

To one side is sage for smudging the room, and Gene explains the symbolism of the act of smudging and how the ritual is a physical representation of clearing the room of negative thoughts and feelings. When a client has breathing or allergy issues, Gene will offer symbolic smudging, without burning the sage. For these times, he will then ask everyone in the room to visualize the smoke rising and taking the negativity with it. On many different levels, this act helps prepare everyone in the room for the storytelling program. You can feel the energy grow calm and relaxed.

This is followed with a two-minute guided meditation that two clients will voluntarily read in tandem. This guided meditation not only brings additional calmness to the room, but it also takes us all to a deeper spiritual level in preparation for the storytelling.

On the other side of the shrine is a basket of rocks—all with their own stories to tell. Some of the rocks come from our walks; others are gifts from friends who know about the basket and its use at Homeward Bound. Although most are left in their original rough form, a few have been polished by Gene. Many come from a variety of locations around the globe, including Peru, Nepal, England, Australia, Greece, and Japan. Some came from sacred locations, and the designation of sacred may be very distinct to the one who first picked up the rock and brought it to us. At the end of every program, the basket of rocks is passed around the room for anyone who wants one to make a selection. Over and over we see that this gesture proves quite significant to the client. Many recognize the symbolism of the rock, although the symbolism varies from person to person.

Between the smudging/meditation and the passing out of the rocks, there are the stories. Because clients come and go on daily basis, the dynamics of the group change from week to week. So in addition to stories that we hope mesh with the Cognitive Behavior Therapy each client receives, we also choose stories that tackle special issues or problems a particular group of clients may be dealing with at that specific time. For example, if flaring tempers are a problem, we may be asked to share a story that addresses anger. "The Tale of Prince Llywelyn and His Faithful Dog Gelert" from Wales or "The Lady of Nam Xuong" from Vietnam are prime examples. A favorite story of forgiveness for this particular group is the Haitian folktale "One, My Darling, Come to Mama." A version of this can be found in Diane Wolkstein's *The Magic Orange Tree and Other Haitian Folktales* (Alfred A. Knopf, 1978). The classic "Lion's Whisker" gets told when we are asked for a story about patience. Although the more common version of this story tells of a woman hoping to subdue the anger of a husband just returned from war, we opt to share the Ethiopian tale of a woman wanting to win over the love of her stepson. This is because many of the female participants (and a few of the males as well) are not only recovering from drug abuse but also domestic violence. A stepson version can be found in *The Lion's Whiskers and Other Ethiopian Tales* by Brent Ashabranner and Russell Davis (Linnet Books, 1997).

By 2015, Gene had been offering storytelling programs at Homeward Bound for 20 years and Peggy for 15 years. We loved what we were doing, and feedback from both clients and personnel was affirming that we were on the right path. There were requests from the Men's and Women's Units to start storytelling sessions for them as well, but our budget just could not allow for carving out any more time from our schedule.

A brainstorming session with a Homeward Bound staff member and volunteer clients proved to be the next game-changer. The Statewide client participants emphasized not only how meaningful the storytelling sessions were for them but also how much they learned from them when it came to telling their own personal stories. Were there any changes with the storytelling program they would like to see? Many expressed the desire to learn how to be better storytellers themselves in order to share their tale of recovery in hopes of helping others. Now with tangible evidence in hand and a new staff member added to ease the burden on Homeward Bound's only grant-writer, we were approached about the possibility of offering storytelling training at the close of 2015 with the intent of providing us some financial remuneration for our time and expenses through grant opportunities that had recently opened up.

At the start of 2016, Homeward Bound offered what was first called the "Storytelling Project" two Monday evenings a month as part of its Recovery Support Services (RSS). Homeward Bound describes what it commonly refers to as RSS: "Recovery coaches assist clients throughout their stay with us and as inpatient treatment is coming to an end. It is the recovery coach who helps with re-entry into the world, finding community resources to help with housing, medical care, and job training." Initially we were coaching the coaches, those who were in longtime recovery and understood firsthand the battles the newly recovering would be facing. They wanted help with telling their stories as a way of dropping the barriers between them and the clients they were wanting to help. As part of the grant requirement, the "Storytelling Project" was open to anyone in service to recovery who wanted to improve their story.

At that first January 2016 meeting, we had four recovery coaches on hand, ready and anxious to not only hone their own storytelling skills but also be a part of a creative and unique recovery program for the state of Texas. Over the first couple of months, our enthusiastic coaches began spreading the gospel of storytelling, and a few new participants began trickling in.

The process is a simple one. At the beginning, we talk about the basics of what storytelling is, story arcs, the hero/heroine's journey, and techniques to capture and hold their audience's attention. Because each story is followed up with a critique from the listeners, we ask everyone to offer one positive point about the story told and one thing the storyteller could do to improve his or her story. The latter could include physical motions, vocal quality, and verbal mannerisms, along with any issue with the actual story itself.

The tellers are also encouraged to hone their stories so they can recount their tale—or a distinct part of their tale—of recovery in approximately 8–12 minutes. They are accustomed to the untimed accounts of sobriety that are shared as part of the Alcoholics Anonymous/Narcotics Anonymous meetings they attend with great regularity. But when asked how many times do they find themselves checking the time after a story has gone longer than 15 minutes, 20 minutes, or 30 minutes, we get the same answer: a room full of grimaces and bobbing heads. To be clear, we do not insist that every teller keep to this time constraint. New members to the group often struggle with this for their first, and often second, telling. And some have such complex stories that constraining them to this amount of time could prove impossible. But it is a goal to work for, and once achieved and with more polished skill, we encourage some to expand their stories or to create a series of vignettes to pick and choose from depending on the situation and audience they want to address.

A requirement of the state arts grant was to host public performances in the greater community. One block from Homeward Bound stands Cliff Temple Baptist Church with a congregation that welcomes and supports Homeward Bound's clients. Upon learning that we needed a venue for a first public performance, they graciously provided a meeting hall that seated 50 with an excellent sound system as well as coffee and refreshments. For that first performance, over 30 people came to hear the stories of friends, loved ones, and even total strangers.

Our early participants were empowered by the success of this first performance, and word began to spread that the Storytelling Project was not only fun but beneficial as well. We had fingers crossed that we might eventually boast a dozen participants, so we were completely unprepared for quickly booming to as many as 30 attendees at the coaching sessions.

Homeward Bound clients who had advanced in their recovery enough to be assigned a recovery coach heard about the storytelling classes from their coaches and asked to come along. Soon we were not only getting those in long-term recovery but also those still enrolled as clients in the Men's, Women's, and Statewide Units.

We were thrilled to see so much interest but quickly discovered that this popularity created another quandary. This many participants meant some never got a chance to tell, not even once, before they graduated from Homeward Bound and returned home or moved on to transitional housing. Although being at Homeward Bound was not required, getting to our meetings could still be challenging. A number of these clients do not live in Dallas. And even for some of those who do, transportation can be a significant issue. Those without a car living in a car-oriented city with poor public transportation can be hard-pressed to find transportation anywhere.

The obvious solution was to meet every Monday evening. This answer also meant that our time requirements more than doubled. But if that sacrifice was a result of the program proving itself to be even more popular than we had anticipated, this was an obvious choice. We usually average five to six tellers with critiquing afterward in an evening. We have a special cigar box and yellow cards for storytelling hopefuls to submit their names for telling that evening. The performers' names are then drawn at random, with an occasional exception for an experienced member to demonstrate telling their recovery story when a significant number of new members are attending. Any names left in the box by the end of the meeting are saved to be the first tellers the following Monday night.

As these words are written, we are completing our ninth month in the program, and it is remaining popular with the clients and recovery coaches at Homeward Bound. Recognizing that what we have learned here could be applied to other communities, we have rebranded the "Storytelling Project" as Telling Your Personal Experiences (Recovery) or TYPE(R). The feedback we are receiving from personnel has all been positive, and over this brief period, we have only hit a few snags that were quickly remedied.

Although we emphasize to the group that it is best to refrain from profanity, we do not position ourselves as the bad language police. Many of our clients have had a lifetime of horrific experiences and words slip out. We opt to stay silent. But we do occasionally remind the group that if they want to share their story in public locations such as churches, they will need to tone down their language. We generally find that the four-letter words gradually disappear the more they share their story.

Our most significant issue has proved to be the combination of Men's and Women's Units' clients in the room at the same time, a significant portion of whom are under the age of 25. Because of past problems at other Homeward Bound programs, often these groups are not allowed to participate at the same time. At this point we are not at liberty to double our program again in order to have separate men's and women's storytelling sessions. Finally, we had to begin meetings by addressing a few rules about no public displays of affection or inappropriate touching. Also, a technician from each unit is now on hand to help supervise. The threat of no longer being allowed to participate in the storytelling program has proved to be a successful misbehavior deterrent as well.

One thing that needs to be pointed out is that there is a distinction between inappropriate touching and genuine physical and emotional support, often expressed via hugs. We have been surprised to discover that despite the hardships so many of these clients have faced, they have proved to be, by far, one of the most supportive groups we have ever experienced. They are there for each other when a story touches something painful deep inside or when a success merits gleeful celebration.

The next milestone we are anxiously awaiting is the public performance schedule on the group's one-year anniversary. This performance will be hosted at a City of Dallas Cultural Arts Center black box theater that seats an audience of over 100. The event will be publicized via the mainstream media sources, and our wish is that at least half of those attending will not know any of the storytellers that night because this will put us even closer to meeting the rest of our goals for this program. Not only will those on stage polish their stories well enough to have them be considered "performance quality," but their stories will reach out to strangers in hopes that those outside the community of drug and alcohol abuse will understand what addicts must deal with physically and emotionally on a daily basis. When these barriers to understanding begin to fall away, then the healing of both the individual and the community he or she lives in can truly be manifest.

Bibliography

Addiction Issues

Alcoholics Anonymous. *The Big Book, Living Sober*. New York: AA World Services, 2002.

Alcoholics Anonymous. *Twelve Steps and Twelve Traditions*. New York: AA World Services, 2002.

Gabor Maté, M. D. *In the Realm of the Hungry Ghosts: Close Encounters with Addiction*. Berkeley, CA: North Atlantic Books, 2010.

Hari, Johann. *Chasing the Scream: The First and Last Days on the War on Drugs*. New York: Bloomsbury USA, 2016.

Kurtz, Ernest, and Katherine Ketcham. *The Spirituality of Imperfection: Storytelling and the Search for Meaning*. New York: Bantam, 1993.

Storytelling

Frank, Arthur W. *The Wounded Storyteller: Body, Illness and Ethics*, 2nd ed. Chicago: University of Chicago Press, 2013.

Meade, Erica Helm. *Tell It by Heart: Women and the Healing Power of Story*. Chicago: Open Court Publishing, 1995.

Meade, Michael. *Men and the Water of Life: Initiation and the Tempering of Men*. San Francisco: HarperSanFrancisco, 1994.

Niemi, Loren, and Elizabeth Ellis. *Inviting the Wolf In: Thinking about Difficult Stories*. Little Rock, AR: August House, 2001.

Story Collections

Ashabranner, Brent, and Russel Davis. *The Lion's Whiskers and Other Ethiopian Tales*. North Haven, CT: Linnet Books, 1997.

Cox, Allison M., and David H. Albert. *The Healing Heart for Communities: Storytelling for Strong and Healthy Communities*. Gabriola Island, BC, Canada: New Society Publishers, 2003.

De Mello, Anthony. *The Song of the Bird*. New York: Image Books, 1984.

Feldman, Christina, and Jack Kornfield. *Stories of the Spirit, Stories of the Heart*. New York: HarperCollins, 1991.

Kornfield, Jack. *Soul Food: Stories to Nourish the Spirit and the Heart*. New York: HarperOne, 1996.

MacDonald, Margaret Read. *Peace Tales: World Folk Tales to Talk About*. Little Rock, AR: August House, 2006.

Meade, Erica Helm. *The Moon in the Well: Wisdom Tales to Transform Your Life, Family and Community*. Chicago: Open Court Publishing, 2001.

Ragan, Kathleen, ed. *Fearless Girls, Wise Women and Beloved Sisters: Heroines in Folktales from Around the World*. New York: W.W. Norton, 2000.

Ragan, Kathleen, ed. *Outfoxing Fear: Folktales from around the World*. New York: W.W. Norton, 2006.

Wolkstein, Diane. *The Magic Orange Tree and Other Haitian Folktales*. New York: Alfred A. Knopf, 1978.

And an assortment of multicultural folktale collections such as Jane Yolen's *Favorite Folktales from around the World* (Random House, 1988).

Bibliography

Books

Cashman, Ray. *Storytelling on the Northern Irish Border: Characters and Community*. Reprint edition. Bloomington, IN: Indiana University Press, 2011.

Cox, Alison M., and David H. Albert. *The Healing Heart for Communities: Storytelling for Strong and Healthy Communities (Families)*. Gabriola Island, BC, Canada: New Society Publishers, 2009.

Fields, Anne M., and Karen R. Diaz. *Fostering Community through Digital Storytelling: A Guide for Academic Libraries*. Westport, CT: Libraries Unlimited, 2008.

Lambert, Joe. *Digital Storytelling: Capturing Lives, Creating Community (Digital Imaging and Computer Vision)*, 4th rev. ed. Abingdom, United Kingdom: Routledge, 2012.

Solinger, Rickie, Madeline Fox, and Kyhan Irani, eds. *Telling Stories to Change the World: Global Voices on the Power of Narrative to Build Community and Make Social Justice Claims*. New York: Routledge, 2008.

Zipes, Jack. *Creative Storytelling: Building Community / Changing Lives*. Abingdom, United Kingdom: Routledge, 1995.

Journal Articles

Gussie, Fauntleroy. "Realm of the Storytellers." *Native Peoples Magazine* 25, no. 3 (2012, May/June): 30–35, 6p.

National Geographic. "Pine Ridge Community Storytelling Project: A Partnership with Cowbird." http://ngm.nationalgeographic.com/2012/08/pine-ridge/community-project-intro.

New Home: The Community Journal. *communityjournal.org*. The Community Journal is a storytelling platform dedicated to sharing stories that break down barriers to knowing and supporting each other.

Storytelling Magazine

Alston, Tina. "Exploring Feelings through Storyimaging." *Storytelling Magazine*, May 1995: 12–14.

Andreas, Brian. "Community-building. Building Community, StoryPeople, and Dreams." *Storytelling Magazine*, September 1996: 4–5.

Duchin, Jason. "Making Dreams Come True." *Storytelling Magazine*, July 1995: 4–5.

Geer, Richard Owen. "Jack Finds Eden: A Community Storytelling/Theatre Project Brings It All Back Home." *Storytelling Magazine*, January/February 2002: 20–22.

Henegar, Steven. "Storybridge: The Stagebridge Senior Storytellers Program." *Storytelling Magazine*, January/February 2002: 17–19.

May, Jim. "Community Wisdom Keepers." *Storytelling Magazine*, January/February 2006: 12–13.

May, Rollo. "Roots of Our Being." *Storytelling Magazine*, Fall 1991: 16–19.

O'Halloran, Susan. "Compassionate Action through Storytelling." *Storytelling Magazine / Storytelling World*, July/August 2000: 24–26.

Pinho, Nicole. "Tales of Tolerance." *Storytelling Magazine*, March/April 2002: 39–41.

Rudd, Connie. "Compelling Stories." *Storytelling Magazine*, January/February 2003: 15–16.

Scott, Susan. "Troubling the Waters: Restoration in the 'Bad Water' Town." *Storytelling Magazine*, September/October 2003: 34–37.

Shannon, Marilyn. "Dayton Stories Project Unites Community." *Storytelling Magazine*, March 1997: 7.

Sima, Judy. "Making Connections: School, Community, and Beyond." *Storytelling Magazine*, November/December 2007: 31–32.

Veterans Education Project. "Community Voices against Violence and Substance Abuse Project." *Storytelling Magazine*, November/December 2007: 18.

Online Resources

"Brimstone Award for Applied Storytelling." Taking its name from brimstone, the elusive element medieval chemists believed would transform base metals into gold, this award focuses on the transformational properties of storytelling and aims to increase understanding of the ways storytelling can promote change in individuals and communities. http://www.storynet.org/grants/brimstone.html.

Berkowitz, Doriet. *Oral Storytelling Building Community through Dialogue, Engagement, and Problem Solving.* http://www.naeyc.org/tyc/files/tyc/file/V5I2/Oral%20Storytelling.pdf.

Ganley, Barbara. "Re-Weaving the Community, Creating the Future: Storytelling at the Heart and Soul of Healthy Communities." Copyright © 2010 by the Orton Family Foundation. https://www.orton.org/resources/storytelling_essay.

Gillard, Marni. "On Building Community through Storytelling." Activities for building a community of learners through story. http://marnigillard.com/storytelling/articles/community.html.

Learning to Give. Lesson plans, complementary folktales, and parent resources to involve students in serving their communities. http://www.learningtogive.org/.

Myrick, Anne Michelle. "Folktales and Philanthropy—Using Folktales as a Bridge to Community Service." SIT Graduate Institute/SIT Study Abroad DigitalCollections@SIT. http://digitalcollections.sit.edu/cgi/viewcontent.cgi?article=1698&context=ipp_collection.

National Storytelling Network. National Storytelling Network Blog. http://blog.storynet.org.

Finnerty, Megan. "How to Make Everything in Your Community Better By Yourself."

Knutson, Katie. "Storytelling: Community through…Competition?"

Marshall, Cindy Rivka. "Hear Our Voices."

Pang, Lilli. "Our Stories, Our Community: Foundation Approach to Storytelling in Communities."

Orton Family Foundation. "Resilience: Using Storytelling in Community Heart & Soul." http://www.resilience.org/resource-detail/2911378-using-storytelling-in-community-heart#.

Stephen, Bradley. "The Power of Community Storytelling." *WIRED*, http://www.wired.com/insights/2014/01/power-community-storytelling/.

Story for All. "Building Community through Stories." http://storyforall.org/StoryBridges.org/Welcome.html.

Wolf, James ("Brother Wolf"). "The Art of Storytelling Podcasts." http://www.artofstorytellingshow.com/past-guests/.

Interview #084 Kim Weitkamp. "Reaching Troubled Youth through Storytelling."

Interview #092 Christine Carlton and Jenni Cargill. "2 Australian Storytellers—Examining the Skeletons in the Cultural Closet."

Interview #093 Gail Herman. "Building a Student Storytelling Festival."

Interview #098 Ben Nind. "Storytelling Is Essential to Community Health."

Interview #099 Emil Wolfgang. "Carrying the Pacific Island Storytelling Culture Forward."

Interview #107 Laird Schaub. "The Application of Story to Group Facilitation and Community Living."

Index

Abdul-Malik, Sarai, 73
Addiction recovery community, storytelling in, 147–53
Adichie, Ngozi, 4
Alcoholics Anonymous, 151
Annual Willingboro Kwanzaa Fest, 72–73
Applied storytelling, 66
Apprenticeship program, 80
Arizona Republic, 99
Art, 79
Artist as Community Cultural Ambassador: A How-To-Guide (Abdul-Malik), 75
Arts-Us Young Storytellers, 82
Ashabranner, Brent, 150
Asian Voices Festival, 15
At-risk youth
    group sessions for, 138–40
    stories for reaching, 134–40
Atwater, Ken, 93

Basting, Anne, 141
Bilingual Nursing Program Mentorship Project (SMCC), 96
Bilingual stories, 38
Birch, Carol, 129
"Blackstorytelling," 72
Blue, Jerry, 82
Blues, 71–72
BlueScope Steel, 38
Books, and stories, 81
B.O.Y.D., 74
Brave New Voices Network of Youth Speaks, 8
Brother Blue, 68, 82
Brunson, Kendall, 69

"Bubba and the Boogie Man," 85–87
Burlington County Board of Freeholders, 74

Calbow, Lorraine, 91–92
Campbell, Joseph, 2
Capoeira, Axe, 98
CaptureHits Marketing Group, 16
Carroll, Thomas, 69
Carter, Melvin, III, 83
Carter, W. Toni, 82
Centenarians, 50–51
Challed, Judy, 55
Champions of Change, 67
Characters, in stories, 43
Chavis, David M., 59
Children at the Well (C@W) storytelling program
    coaching in, 8–12
    funding, 12
    organization and management, 5–7
    students, 6
    transforming society through, 2–13
Choudhury, Arif, 19
Civil War, 83
Claymont Elementary, 31–35
Coaching staff
    role in C@W program, 6
    storytelling styles at C@W program, 8–12
Coggswell, Gladys, 51
College-based storytelling program, and community, 91–101
Columbus Story Adventures (CSA) program, 102–8
    First Book and, 104

sample activity, 108
"Story Soup" fund-raiser, sample
    invitation for, 107
Comer, Beverly, 102–3
Community building, 58
    authentic, 61–64
    and folk art, 59
    and funders, 62
    international and storytelling,
        23–36
    and stories, 59
    and story programs, 61–64
    through college-based storytelling
        program, 91–101
    through cultural storytelling,
        82–85
    and time-related challenges, 62
Community leaders, 62
Community voice, 61–62
Cordi, Kevin, 124
Cotter, Michael, 55
Crandall, Sally, 102–3
Creative placemaking, 67
Creative Placemaking, 67
Creative story
    for Alzheimer's patients, 141–46
    compensation, 144
    materials needed, 144
    for those with other special needs,
        141–46
Creative Story Project, 141
Cultural storytelling, and building
    community, 82–85
Cultural sustainability, 66
    and storytelling, 67
Cyrus, Jill, 69

*Dancing at the Crossroads: A Guide
    for Practitioners in At-Risk
    Programming: Stories of Choice
    and Empowerment,* 139
The Danger of the Single Story, 4
Davis, Donald, 92, 98
Davis, Russell, 150
Davis-McGee, Adam, 83
Degree-seeking students, 94–95
Delta Sigma Theta Inc., 74
Denton, Doug, 148
Digital program, 46
Director(s)
    role in C@W program, 5–6
Discrimination stories, 16
Dowd Center program, 105
Doyle, Don, 92

Ducey, Mary Gay, 92
Dudding, Kate, 3

Education
    parental involvement in child's, 38
    workshop, 37–47
Elders
    centenarians, 50–51
    Circle, 54–57
    and Eldertel program, 51–52
    and Illinois Storytelling Inc.,
        55–56
    storytelling, 50–57
Eldertel program, 51–52
Elliott, Doug, 92
Ellis, Elizabeth, 92
Ellis, Rex, 92
Elsner, Paul, 93
Emancipation Proclamation, 87
Entwisle, D. R., 102
Euro Americans, 77, 80
Evenson, Kris, 16–17
Expressions, 44

Facebook, 17–18, 51
Family, Fun & Folklife Workshop
    Series, 66
    applied storytelling in, 66
    audience, 73–74
    community collaborators, 74–75
    creative placemaking in, 67
    cultural sustainability, 66
    design phases, 69–73
    funding, 74
    goals, 68
    and need for storytellers, 67–68
    objectives, 69
    scope, 68
    social entrepreneurship, 66
Family Adventures in Reading
    (FAIR) program, 21–22
Family Alliance, 56
Federal Bureau of Investigation
    (FBI), 33
Ferlatte, Diane, 92
Fiasco, Lupe, 71
Finnerty, Megan, 99
First Book, 104
Flewellyn, Valada Parker, 82
Folk art, and community building,
    59
Folktales and myths, 78
Ford, Lynette, 92, 98, 102–3
Forrest, Heather, 92

Frisco Independent School District
     (FISD), 109–10
Frisco Public Library Foundation,
     109
Frisco Storytelling Festival. *See*
     Lone Star Storytelling Festival
The Frog Who Wanted to Be a Singer
     (Goss), 82

Galloway, Alanna Carter, 84
Galloway, Anthony, 85–87
Games, 44
Ganz, Marshall, 96
Georgia Sea Island Singers, 83
Gladden House, 105
Goodwill or Salvation Army, 79
Goss, Linda, 82
Greater Columbus Arts Council, 102
Gullah people, 83

Handley, Leslie, 52–53
Heritage Night
     School Programming, 127–31
The Hickey Interfaith Center of
     Nazareth College, 8
Hip hop, 71–72
Hispanic Coalition, 105
Historic Rock Castle, 60–61
Holley, Shelley, 109
Homeless Families Foundation, 105
Homeward Bound, Dallas, 147–53
Homeward Bound Inc., 147–48

I am Kenny J Productions, 74
Illinois Arts Council, 54
Illinois Department on Aging, 55
Illinois Storytelling Festival. *See*
     Illinois Storytelling Inc. (ISI)
Illinois Storytelling Inc. (ISI),
     54–55
     first Elders Circle, 55
     first training workshops, 55
     invitations to elders for school
       visits, 55–56
In FACT Inc., 68, 74
Intercultural understanding, 37–47
     and expression, 44
     and games, 44
     and language, 44
     program structure outline, 38–39
     program structure with detail,
       39–47
     and stories, 40–42
     and storytellers, 40–42

Interfaith Story Circle, 2–3
Interfaith Youth Core, 8
Intergenerational knowledge,
     37–47
     and bilingual stories, 38
     and expression, 44
     and games, 44
     and language, 44
     and stories, 40–42
     and storytellers, 40–42
Intergenerational storytelling, 51–52
International Center of the Capital
     Region, 7

Jaliya, 72
Jennings, Jacqueline, 69
Johnson, Gert, 2–3, 5
Joy, Flora, 124
JustStories Festival, 15, 17

Kaleidoscope
     Valuing Differences and Creating
       Inclusion curriculum, 16
Kawambe-Omowale Drum and
     Dance Theatre, 98
Keepers of the Culture Inc., 74
*Kirkwood as It Was (1895–1929):
     Meramec Highlands,* 52–53
Kirkwood Historical Society, 52
Klein, Susan, 92
Kumbayah—the Juneteenth Story,
     86

Lacapa, Michael, 92
"The Lady of Nam Xuong," 150
Language, 44
LGBTQ community, 100
Lincoln, Abraham, 86
LinkedIn, 18
"Lion's Whisker," 150
*The Lion's Whiskers and Other
     Ethiopian Tales* (Ashabranner
     and Davis), 150
Lipman, Doug, 92
"Little Weapon," 71
Lone Star Storytelling Festival, 109
     after, 115–16
     audience, 110
     auditions and judging, 111–12
     community collaboration and
       funding of, 109
     concerts, 113–15
     history of, 109
     program scope, 109–10

Lone Star Student Storyteller
    Program, 109–22
  anecdotes/quotes, 118
  audience, 110
  auditions and judging, 111–12
  coaching sessions, 113
  community collaboration and
    funding of, 109
  concerts, 113–15
  history of, 109
  orientation, 112–13
  orientation, coaching sessions
    and special performances,
    121–22
  publicity, 110–11
  sample orientation documents,
    119–20
  school partnership, 110
  scope, 109–10
Loya, Olga, 92

*The Magic Orange Tree and Other
  Haitian Folktales* (Wolkstein),
  150
MariSol Federal Credit Union, 96
Markusen, Ann, 67
Markut, Lynda, 55
May, Jim, 55, 92
McDonald, Margaret Read, 92
McMillan, David W., 59
Memorization skills, 44–45
Memory Makers, 55
Mesa Arts Center (MAC), 99
Minnesota Humanities Center, 86
Missouri Arts Council, 52
Missouri Folk Arts Program, 51
Missouri Humanities
  Council, 52
MMC Starlight GRC Ltd., 29
The Moth, 50
Multicultural Communities
  Council, 38
Multicultural live performances,
  14–15
Myth-Mob, 97

Narcotics Anonymous, 151
National Association of Black
  Storytellers, 15
National Association of Black
  Storytellers Festival,
  Philadelphia, 82
National Council of Teachers of
  English (NCTE), 51

National Endowment for the Arts,
  67, 81
National Endowment for the
  Humanities, 81
National Geographic, 79
National Parks Service, 66
National Storytelling Network
  (NSN), 3, 18, 74
National Storytelling Youth
  Olympics, 124
National Youth Storytelling Hall of
  Fame, 124
National Youth Storytelling
  Showcase (NYSS), 123–26
  mission, 123
  vision, 123–26
Nation of Islam Willingboro Study
  Group, 74
A New Pair of Wings, 81
Nicodemus, Anne Gadwa, 67
Norfolk, Bobby, 92, 98
Nyberg, John, 60–61

Obama, Barack, 77
O'Callahan, Jay, 92
Ologboni, Tejumola, 82
Olson, L. L., 102
"One, My Darling, Come to Mama,"
  150
Online storytelling festival, 17
Overholser, Lisa, 23–24, 28–31

Panafest International Storytelling
  Festival, Ghana, 82
Panel discussions, 79
Pang, Lillian Rodrigues, 38
Parenting magazine, 54
Parent Teacher Organization
  (PTO), 53
Paul G. Duke Foundation, 103
Performance pieces, 46
Personal object story, 128
Personal stories, 78
Pinterest, 18
Probe, Marilyn, 51
Project TELL (Teaching English
  through Living Language),
  52–53
Puppets, 42–43

Raanan, Yoram, 2
RaceBridges Studio, 17
Rachel Muha's Run the Race
  Program, 105

Racism, 14, 78, 81
Radner, Jo, 19
Read aloud, 22
Reading, and multicultural family
    adventures, 21–22
Reagan-Blake, Connie, 92
"Red Altar," 78, 79, 81
Reed, Caroliese Frink, 72
Reference displays, 22
Regan-Blake, Connie, 98
Robert Wood Johnson
    Foundation, 96
Rocha, Antonio, 92, 98
Rose, Elizabeth, 124

Sacre, Antonio, 14, 92
Satellite Elders Circles, 55
Schwartz, Cherie Karo, 2
"Sense of Community," 59
"Signifying Monkey," 83
Simons, Father Derek, 14–17
Smith, Mother Mary Carter, 82
Social entrepreneurship, 66
Social justice storytelling, 14–20
    challenges, 18
    festival, 15–16
    marketing, 18
    multicultural live performances,
        14–15
    online storytelling festival, 17
    statistics, 19
    videotaping discrimination and
        triumphs stories, 16
    videotaping professional tellers'
        social justice stories, 17
Society of The Divine Word, 14
South Mountain Community
    College (SMCC). See
    Storytelling Institute (South
    Mountain Community College)
Special events, 80
Stenson, Jane, 19
St. John Learning Center, 106
St. John's Episcopal Church, 103
St. Louis Regional Arts
    Commission, 52
St. Louis Storytelling Festival,
    28–31, 50
St. Louis Storytelling Festival
    Advisory Committee, 23
Stories
    becoming visible through, 77–81
    and community building, 59
    elements of, 42–43

history, 78–79
and intercultural understanding,
    40–42
and intergenerational knowledge,
    40–42
personal, 78
personal object, 128
for reaching at-risk youth, 134–40
Story, Naomi, 93
Story Power program, of Creative
    Story Project, 141
Story programs, and community
    building, 61–64
Storytellers
    as community cultural
        ambassadors, 66–75
    and intercultural understanding,
        40–42
    and intergenerational knowledge,
        40–42
    need for, 67–68
Storytellers of Central Ohio, 102–8
Storytelling
    in the addiction recovery
        community, 147–53
    applied, 66
    building international community
        through, 23–36
    certificate students, 95–96
    and community building, 59–64
    and cultural sustainability, 67
    elders, 50–57
    and identity, 47
Storytelling Institute (South
    Mountain Community College),
    91–101
    Bilingual Nursing Program
        Mentorship Project, 96
    commitment to diversity, 99–100
    community interest, 97
    degree-seeking students, 94–95
    faculty training, 93–94
    faculty who are storytellers and
        their development, 91–94
    future of, 100–101
    internal and external
        partnerships, 98–99
    quality programming, 97–98
    storytelling certificate students,
        95–96
    student-centered curriculum with
        artistic and academic integrity,
        94–97
Storytelling Magazine, 18

St. Stephens Community
House, 106
Students
degree-seeking, 94–95
storytelling certificate, 95–96
Sustainability, cultural, 66

"Takashi's Dream," 78
"The Tale of Prince Llywelyn and
His Faithful Dog Gelert," 150
Talk-back discussion, 22
Talk That Talk (Goss and Barnes),
82
Tandem telling, 42
Target, 103
Tennessee Arts Commission, 62
Texas Commission on the Arts, 147
This American Life, 50
Thomas, Winnie, 70
Thrivent Financial for Lutherans,
103–4
TIDE Conference of YouthLead, 8
Time*Slips,* 141
Torrance, Jackie, 92
Torres, Marilyn, 94, 96, 98
"Tribes & Bridges," 14
Triumphs' stories, 16
Tuskegee Airmen, 54
Twitter, 18, 51

Underground Railroad of
Burlington County, 74
University of Missouri Extension,
28–31

Videotaping
discrimination and triumphs
stories, 16

professional tellers' social justice
stories, 17
Voice, 44

Walker, Richard, 54
Washington, Donna, 92
*Water Spider Brings Fire to the
Animals,* 58
Watts, Nannette, 124
"Weaving Community" program,
59–61
environment, 63
funding, 62
simplistic program, 63
Weir, Liz, 92
*Whole Story Handbook: Using
Imagery to Complete the Story
Experience* (Birch), 129
Williams, La'Ron, 14
Willingboro Garden
Association, 74
Willingboro Recreation Center, 69
Wills, Aaron, 31–35
Wills, Allison, 35–36
Wojciechowicz, LynnAnn, 93
Wolfgramm, Emil, 92
Wolkstein, Diane, 150
Wong, Joey, 23, 24–28
Woodstock Opera House, 56
Woolery, Lee Ann, 50
Workshops, 37–47, 79–80

YouTube, 50
YWCA, 81

Zeta Phi Beta Sorority Inc., 74
Zulu, Elder Nothando, 82
Zulu, Vusi, 82

About the Editors and Contributors

About the Editors

Jane Stenson and Sherry Norfolk are the coauthors of the award-winning *The Storytelling Classroom: Applications across the Curriculum* (Libraries Unlimited, 2006) and *Literacy Development in the Storytelling Classroom* (Libraries Unlimited, 2009) as well as two other books on storytelling strategies for education.

Sherry Norfolk is an award-winning storyteller, author, and teaching artist, performing and leading residencies and professional development workshops nationally and internationally. As a performing artist, she is a dynamic storyteller, telling well-crafted and age-appropriate folktales from around the world. As a teaching artist, she uses storytelling as a strategy for teaching pre-K–12th-grade curriculum. Coauthor of The Storytelling Classroom series (four books that explore rigorous, standards-based storytelling strategies for learning across the curriculum) and an adjunct professor at Lesley University, she is a recognized leader in integrating learning through storytelling. E-mail: shnorfolk@aol.com; www.sherrynorfolk.com.

Jane Stenson is a storyteller, storytelling teaching artist, and educator. She has written and edited numerous books—The Storytelling Classroom series—and articles on the use of storytelling in the classroom and is a leading authority on integrated learning through storytelling. Jane serves as cochair of the Youth, Educators, & Storytellers Alliance (YES!), a special interest group of the National Storytelling Network (NSN). In 2016, she received the Distinguished National Service Award from NSN, recognizing her dedicated years of teaching service in storytelling and education. E-mail: www.janestenson.com stenson.stories@gmail.com.

About the Contributors

Karen Abdul-Malik, artistically known as "Queen Nur," is an international storyteller, teaching artist, and folklorist. She is the founder and executive director of In FACT Inc.: Innovative Solutions through Folk Art, Culture and Tradition, a cultural sustainability organization designed to create opportunities for civic engagement through folklife traditions. Karen is a winner of the MidAtlantic Artist-As-Catalyst Award; the NSN Brimstone Grant; and several leadership awards. She has a MA in Cultural Sustainability, Goucher College; BS in Criminal Justice, Northeastern University; and, Certificate of Dispute Resolution, Harvard Law School. Queen is the 14th president of the National Association of Black Storytellers Inc. and is the upcoming folklore director at Perkins Center for the Arts. Recordings include Parent's Choice Winner "Sweet Potato Pie and Such" and "Live and Storified." Karen has authored *What Is the Role of Storytelling in Cultural Sustainability? Four Case Studies* and *Artist as Community Cultural Ambassador: A How-To-Guide*. E-mail: infactorg@gmail.com; websites: www.queennur.com; www.innovativefact.org.

Cherri Coleman is a curriculum designer and teacher of dance, theatre, storytelling, and heritage arts. Graduates of her student-led performing arts programs have gone on to Broadway, international tours, careers in stage-craft and graphic arts, video, music, and film. Cherri, a native Tennessean, also keeps alive local traditions of storytelling and white oak and cane basketry, training the next generation of heritage art enthusiasts. Her current endeavors include "Celebrating Our Roots"©, which partners with the National Storytelling Network and local historic sites to train high school and middle school students in leadership, community building and historic preservation, and "Math and the Art of Basketry"—a hands-on exploration of geometry through visual art. Cherri served on the board of directors of the National Storytelling Network and is a member of Artist Corps Tennessee.

Lorna MacDonald Czarnota is an award-winning storyteller and author of the three-book series Dancing at the Crossroads, which includes *Stories and Activities for At-Risk Youth Programming, A Guide for Caregivers in At-Risk Programs*, and *A Guide for Practitioners in At-Risk Youth Programming*. She holds a bachelor's degree in Creative Studies for Young Children, master's in Special Education, and certification in Trauma Counseling. Lorna is the founder of Crossroads Story Center Inc., a not-for-profit for reaching at-risk youth through story, working with abused women and children, runaway and homeless youth, and communities in crisis. Storytelling: *www.storyhavenstudio.com*; At-Risk Youth: www.crossroadsstorycenter.com; E-mail: *Lczarnota@aol.com*.

Lynnette (Lyn) Ford is an author, itinerant storyteller, and teacher artist with the Ohio Alliance for Arts Education and the Kennedy Center's Ohio State-Based Collaborative Initiative. Lyn is also a mentor for Thurber House's summer writing camps for young authors and a contributor to several education resources, including *Literacy Development in the Storytelling Classroom, The Storytelling Classroom: Applications across the Storytelling Curriculum*, and *Social Studies in the Storytelling Classroom: Exploring Our Cultural Voices and Perspectives*. Lyn's latest publication for families with young children is *Boo-Tickle Tales: Not-So-Scary Stories for Ages 4-9*, written with friend and fellow storyteller Sherry Norfolk.

Frisco Public Library Frisco Public Library's team of contributors has over 30 years of collective experience producing community storytelling programs. Our writing team includes the current producer of the Lone Star Storytelling Festival and assistant director—Library Public Services, Mayra Diaz. Jennifer Cummings, Youth Services manager, oversees the Lone Star

Storytellers student program each year with help from Youth Services librarians Bonnie Barber, Cindy Boatfield, and Lisa Bubert and Youth Services library assistant Julie Chappell. Each contributor serves as a storytelling coach and shares the labor of love that is taking students' stories from infancy to stage stars each year.

Gene Helmick-Richardson After earning his PhD in entomology, Gene took a 10-year career detour into historical museum reenactment. It was at the Georgia Agrirama and Homeplace 1850 at the Land between the Lakes where he honed his skills as a storyteller and historical agricultural/folklife interpreter. After a brief return to the field of entomology, Gene could not resist the siren's call of storytelling. In 1999, he was appointed to the board of the Tejas Storytelling Association and served as president in 2002. He is currently president of the Dallas Storytelling Guild and has served on that organization's board for a number of years. Gene also served as site director for the Texas Storytelling Festival for over 10 years. In addition to telling stories as a member of Twice upon a Time, he can sometimes be heard spinning tales as Mr. Kennedy, the 1870s farmer at Dallas Heritage Village.

Peggy Helmick-Richardson Prior to joining Gene on the professional storytelling stage in 1999, Peggy was an award-winning reporter and freelance writer. She has a BS in biology and a master's degree in journalism. On the board of the Dallas Storytelling Guild since 2003, Peggy served as president of the nonprofit storytelling organization in 2004 and 2012. Over the years, Peggy has produced a number of story concerts, including Sacred Tales for the Texas Storytelling Festival. She continues to write for the *Allen Image*, edited the 2008 Healing Storytelling Alliance journal *Diving in the Moon*, and contributed a chapter to *Team Up! Tell in Tandem*. Peggy also writes the blog twicetellerstales.

Jim May is an Emmy award-winning storyteller, teacher, and author of the critically acclaimed *Farm on Nippersink Creek* and a children's picture book, *The Boo Baby Meets the Ghost of Mable's Gable*. A professional storyteller for over 25 years, Jim has told stories to all ages across the United States and in Canada and Europe.

Rose McGee, MEd, is coauthor of the recently published book *Story Circle Stories* and author of the plays *Kumbayah...The Juneteenth Story* and *Sleep with a Virgin...A Perspective on AIDS*. For over a decade, she coached the awarding-winning Arts-Us Young Storytellers—the first youth group to perform in the National Black Storytellers Festival. As an educator, she helps teachers understand the power of integrating storytelling into curriculum. Her work with the Minnesota Humanities allows her to use a creative approach to professional development and community engagement with focus on the powerful impact that storytelling, story circles, and integrating the arts into curriculum have in relationship building. Rose created community-building concepts, like Sweet Potato Comfort Pie, Headscarf Society, TeaLit, and has a featured TEDx Talk on The Power of Pie. She is featured in the 2015 National PBS television documentary, *A Few Good Pie Places*. Rose is a 2015 recipient of the Minnesota Social Impact Center's Change Maker Award and resides in Golden Valley, Minnesota.

Onawumi Jean Moss is a storyteller, narrator, keynote speaker, and author. The performances of this talking book and rhythm master encourage pride of heritage, appreciation of cultural differences, and recognition of kinship.

Susan O'Halloran Seen on PBS, *Nightline*, and in the *New York Times*, the *Chicago Reader* says Susan O'Halloran "has mastered the Irish art of telling stories that are funny and heart-wrenching at the same time." Susan has several times been a featured teller at the National Storytelling Festival and the International Storytelling Center Residencies and as a National Storytelling Network keynote speaker. Sue offers webinars on how *not* to offend people of different races and consulting for organizations that want to prevent rather than deal with PR and legal nightmares around race and other diversity dimensions. Websites: www.SusanOHalloran.com; www.RacebridgesStudio.com.

Lisa Overholser, PhD, is a University of Missouri Extension Urban Region community arts specialist and St. Louis Storytelling Festival director. She works with her colleagues in the Community Arts Program to foster arts-based economic and community development for Missouri's citizens. Prior to coming to Missouri, she was the staff folklorist at the New York Folklore Society, a statewide nonprofit organization serving folklife researchers, scholars, practitioners, and artists, where she managed the mentoring and professional development program and directed other folklife programming. She holds a PhD in folklore and ethnomusicology from Indiana University–Bloomington and a MM and BM in piano performance and music history.

Lillian Rodrigues Pang can only be described as a dramatic, involved, and passionate storyteller. She will create worlds and journeys and characters that take over your imagination and win your heart. Lilli tells stories in English and uses a range of languages and instruments to honor the country of origin, so be prepared to clap, dance, sing, creep, and enjoy. Join her and share in the beauty of storytelling at its best. Lilli has travelled Australia and the world performing at the Opera House, Dreaming Festival in Peru, Colombia, Singapore, and many other stages. When the stage lights are not on, she is working consistently with community with current programs in mental health centres, with recently arrived refugees, facilitating Indigenous story gathering and sharing and in disadvantaged regions working on social inclusion and literacy. Website: www.thestoryline.com.au.

Lynn Rubright, professor emerita, Webster University, St. Louis, Missouri, author, and professional storyteller has received a Lifetime Achievement Award and Circle of Excellence Award from the National Storytelling Network. In 2013, she received the St. Louis Outstanding Arts Educator Grand Center Visionary Award. She designed and directed Project TELL (Teaching English through Living Language) for Kirkwood, Missouri, schools; cofounded the Metro Theater Company; and cofounded the St. Louis Storytelling Festival. Her book *Beyond the Beanstalk: Interdisciplinary Learning through Storytelling*'s (Heinemann, 1996) chapters 10, 11, and 12 served as a resource for this chapter. Her children's book, *Mama's Window* (Lee and Low Books, 2005), is used in classrooms studying diversity and civil rights along with the Emmy award-winning video documentary she coproduced: *Oh Freedom after While: The Story of the Sharecroppers in SE Missouri in 1939*. She performs "Little Red the Folktale Hen" as a one-woman musical storytelling event for children and intergenerational audiences.

Pete and Joyce Vanderpool have been involved with storytelling for over 20 years, associated with two different storytelling guilds. They are the founders of Creative Story Project, www.creativestoryproject.com, a nonprofit corporation, dedicated to demonstrating the power of story. They have been members of the Cleveland Storytelling Guild of Cleveland, Tennessee, since 1996. They are also members of the National Storytelling Network and have participated in multiple workshops under the tutelage of such professionals as Donald Davis, Willy Claflin, Kim Weitkamp, Megan Hicks, Doug Lipman, Mary Hamilton, Lyn Ford, and others. Membership in the Alzheimer's Foundation of America (AFA) gives them valuable resources for their work.

Nancy Wang and Robert Kikuchi-Yngojo have shared Eth-Noh-Tec's artistic directorship since 1981. Bringing Nancy's dance, choreography, and theater experience into synthesis with Robert's musical talents, composing and theater experience, their artistry exploded into a unique expression of forms East and West. Eth-Noh-Tec's signature has become a stylized interdisciplinary seamlessness of movement, music, and the spoken word, whether in recounting an age-old folktale or a contemporary statement on modern-day issues of social justice or relationships. Taking this synergism and combining it with their mutual vision of the interplay between the arts and humanities, their performance style embodies the spiritual and the human, the eastern and western, the social and the personal, the traditional and the experimental, broadening their performance spectrum and creating a form and message that is both Asian American and universal in its appeal. They perform around the world and have received numerous grants and awards, including NSN Circle of Excellence and International StoryBridge Award. Website: www.ethnohtec.org.

Liz Warren makes her living telling stories and teaching storytelling as the director of the South Mountain Community College Storytelling Institute. She travels often to Ireland to teach and to learn more about the Celtic stories she specializes in sharing.

Nannette Watts is the executive director of the National Youth Storytelling Showcase. Combining careers in storytelling, choreography, and a degree in Music Dance Theatre, she embraces the world of performing arts. She has been a featured regional teller at Timpanogos Storytelling Festival and festivals from Idaho to Utah's corners. She wrote the first book on running a youth storytelling festival. Author of *Youth Tell*, she encourages leadership training through storytelling programs. Nannette educates people in storytelling and public speaking. She is a highly requested storyteller, story coach, and performing artist. She is the artistic director for Resonance Story Theatre and has worked on the Timpanogos youth storytelling committee for almost two decades. Blending movement and voice, she creates characters that captivate listeners. For more information and to contact see nannettewatts.com.

Paula Weiss is cocreator and director of Children at the Well Youth Storytellers for Peace & Understanding. She came to the world of storytelling through the interest of her daughter Adah, who was 11 at the time. Paula holds a BA from the University of Virginia in Comparative Religion and a CAS in Reading from State University of New York (SUNY) at Albany. She has worked as a switchboard operator, as a teacher, as a research assistant, and in academic editing. In her current position, she uses every one of the skills she developed in those occupations and in the course of her studies.

Paula and her husband Joe Hetko are now the proud parents of two young adults and live in Boght Corners, New York.

Aaron Wills, EdD, has served as the principal at Claymont Elementary School since 2007. Prior to that, he was the principal at Beaufort Elementary School in the Union R-XI School District for five years. He also spent eight years teaching elementary school in first grade, third grade, and fourth grade. He was the Union Distinguished Services Educator of the Year in the spring of 2007 and was presented with the Special Ambassador Award by the Special School District in 2012. He enjoys jazz music and fast-pitch wiffleball.